Pride & Joy:

LGBTQ Artists, Icons and Everyday Heroes

Kathleen Archambeau

Pride & Joy: LGBTQ Artists, Icons and Everyday Heroes

Library of Congress Cataloging
Name: Kathleen Archambeau
Title: Pride & Joy: LGBT Artists, Icons and Everyday Heroes
Library of Congress Control Number: 2017906349
ISBN: (paperback) 978-1-63353-550-3, (ebook) 978-1-63353-551-0
BISAC category code BIO031000 BIOGRAPHY & AUTOBIOGRAPHY / LGBT

Printed in the United States of America

Acknowledgments

Brenda Knight, my publisher extraordinaire. Justin Loeber, Mouth Publicity. John Bowman, first editor. Lisa Haefele Thomas, MS-Word maven. Susan Liroff, Spitfire Graphics. Anna Marks, Oaktown Video. Jay Thomas III, Website designer.

All who agreed to tell their stories with unflinching honesty and passion. Dustin Lance Black, Foreword.

The local bookstores, colleges and universities, nonprofit organizations, public service groups, academics, friends and boosters, thank you. Women's National Book Author's (WNBA) Association, San Francisco Chapter.

My Black Labrador Guide Dog Career Change Puppy who kept me company many long hours of research and writing. My Beloved, without whom none of this would be possible.

"As a producer and literary rep, I have long been committed to inclusion and diversity regarding gender, race, and sexual orientation. My co-authored book, *Dating Your Character,* focuses on helping writers create multi-dimensional, non-stereotypical characters as Kathleen has shown in real-life stories in this extraordinary book. I'm delighted to endorse *Pride & Joy: LGBTQ Artists, Icons and Everyday Heroes,* as it spotlights queer luminaries living open, fulfilling, happy and successful lives—a departure from many LGBTQ portrayals."

Marilyn R. Atlas
Sundance Film Festival Award-Winning Co-Producer,
Real Women Have Curves (HBO)
Co-Author of Dating Your Character (Stairway Press, 2016)

"Kathleen Archambeau wrote a regular column of inspiring profiles for one of the longest-running and largest LGBTQ newspapers in the country, the *San Francisco Bay Times.* We're proud to have been her first public forum. Her book, *Pride & Joy: LGBTQ Artists, Icons and Everyday Heroes,* tells the in-depth stories of 30 global queer icons and is sure to embolden the next generation and give hope to those still struggling with their sexual and gender identity."

Betty Sullivan, PhD
Publisher, San Francisco Bay Times (Founded in 1978)
First LGBT newspaper in California and one of the first in the world

"*Pride & Joy: LGBTQ Artists, Icons and Everyday Heroes* not only highlights the contributions of LGBT citizens to world culture, but shows young queer students that being openly gay can bring you happiness, fulfillment and success. The impact it will have on our next generation, as well as on all those who care about social justice, will be significant."

Mark Leno
First Openly Gay Man Elected to the
California State Senate
Author, SB48, the Fair, Accurate,
Inclusive and Respectful (F.A.I.R.) Education Act (2011):
(Ensures LGBT people and persons
with disabilities are integrated into Education textbooks
and social studies curricula in California public schools)
California State Senator (2008-2016)
California State Assembly (2002-2008)
Candidate for Mayor of San Francisco (Declared, 2017)

"You are amazing! I'm so excited about your book. So proud!"

Libby Schaaf, Mayor of Oakland

Table of Contents

Foreword by
Dustin Lance Black

Academy Award, Best Original Screenplay, *Milk*, 2009

Writer: *J. Edgar*, 2011; *8 the Play*, 2013
ABC TV mini-series creator: *When We Rise*, 2017

Growing up in a conservative, Mormon, military home in San Antonio, Texas, some would say the deck was stacked against me. I knew I was gay from around six years old and was certain that meant I was going to hell. If anyone ever found out, I'd be shunned by my peers and bring great shame to my family. In a massive turn of luck, my mom fell in love with an Army soldier who had orders to ship out to California. We packed up our yellow Malibu Classic and headed West. It was there I first heard the true story of Harvey Milk, an openly gay leader who won at the ballot box by extinguishing fear with hope. Hearing his story literally saved my life.

As a filmmaker working behind the scenes in Hollywood, I could be openly gay and mostly avoid homophobia. So when my screenplay for *Milk* won the Academy Award, I followed my forefathers' and foremothers' examples and shared my own story on the Oscar's massive stage in hopes of sending yet another message of hope to LGBTQ viewers who had been shunned, marginalized, turned out by their families, or condemned by their churches. I ended my speech that night with a wish of my own—that perhaps one day I'd fall in love and get married, too. After half a decade of work as an activist and organizer fighting for marriage equality, I am now engaged to a professional athlete with even greater passion and discipline (not to mention abs) than I will ever have, and we live happily in London together today. My dream has come true. But even with marriage equality won in the US, our larger, global dreams of LGBTQ equality for all are still far from realized.

For too long our stories have been robbed from us, buried in fear and shame. Until recently, we would have been labeled mentally ill or criminal for even claiming our stories as our own. In many countries that is still the case. So diving back into an excavation of our long buried LGBTQ history with ABC's miniseries, *When We Rise*, I gathered a group

Tom Daley, British Olympic diver and his fiancé, Dustin Lance Black, in London, UK

of diverse artists to help tell more of our stories in an even more inclusive fashion. But even this effort only scratches the surface. Far more light must be shed on who we are and where we come from. It is our combined histories, efforts, and stories that help define us as a people, pull us out of isolation, bring us together in community, and inspire us to rise up by reminding us that we have risen before, fought back before, faced backlash before, and won. Sharing our stories and our histories is not an exercise in nostalgia. Our history laid manifest is the foundation of our power.

This book, *Pride & Joy: LGBTQ Artists, Icons and Everyday Heroes*, by longtime LGBTQ activist Kathleen Archambeau, empowers queer youth to do more than survive, but to thrive, whatever the challenges, whatever the losses, whatever the risks, wherever you find yourself. It encourages LGBTQ citizens of the world to live open, happy, fulfilling, strong and successful lives, and utilizes the power of true stories to demonstrate that a brighter, freer future is possible even in what feel like impossible circumstances. The stories told in this book are not simply reflections. Combined and shared, they have the power to help us recognize and fortify our own tremendous strength.

Introduction

I don't want LGBTQ youth coming out to their parents
to experience what I did when my liberal, native San
Franciscan, Irish-American Catholic mother responded,
"I'd love all my children— even if they were murderers,
drug addicts, or prostitutes." She sincerely thought she was
being broad-minded, to which I replied, "Do you realize,
Mom, that you're comparing being gay to being criminal,
mentally ill, or dissolute?" Redemption came that next
Mother's Day when she asked for the book, *Love, Ellen:
A Mother Daughter Journey*, by Betty DeGeneres, instead
of flowers. Identifying with a celebrity mother reconciled
my mother to the fact that her firstborn was a lesbian
and it wasn't the end of the world. I don't want LGBTQ
young professionals to experience what I did as a closeted
lesbian in a corporation where it was literally dangerous
to come out in the early 1980s. In one of my Persuasive
Speaking classes at a Silicon Valley high-technology
company, one of my students, an educated male American
engineer, delivered a speech justifying murder for only five
crimes, one of which was homosexuality. At another tech
company, I was outed by a former friend and colleague
and subsequently fired by a "cracker" CEO. A labor
lawyer advised that I had no recourse since I was not
out and couldn't prove that this was a targeted "layoff."
The next corporate job, I was out to my department, but
not to the salespeople I was training around the world.
When the secretary outed me to the entire building at
corporate headquarters, I had recourse with my boss and
HR because I was out and was, subsequently, promoted,
and the secretary moved to another building with a stern
warning. One night during Pride week in San Francisco's
Castro District, I was walking with my partner and a

group of teenagers taunted us, threatening to attack us when, fortunately, a phalanx of gay men from a nearby bar came out and surrounded us, protecting us from what was sure to become yet another hate crime. When I first met my Kiwi wife, she was not a citizen and we couldn't marry in the US. This caused us to make all kinds of jujitsu moves; from becoming Civil Union partners in New Zealand to carrying Power of Attorney papers everywhere we went to paying extraordinary taxes and tax preparation fees because we could not marry. That was not that long ago: Marriage Equality was just won in the US Supreme Court on June 26, 2015.

The Human Rights Campaign (HRC) found that 53 percent of Americans are still closeted at work ("The Cost of the Closet and The Rewards of Inclusion," HRC, 5/7/14). Within the US, twenty states still have no legal protections against employment discrimination based on sexual orientation, and four other states have no legal protections except for state employees. Only twenty states offer full employment protection based on sexual orientation and gender identity. Since the Human Rights Campaign has assessed corporations through its Corporate Equality Index (CEI), 92 percent of the *Fortune 500* prohibit employment discrimination based on sexual orientation and 199 scored 100 percent, while 327 of the *Fortune 500* scored 91 percent or higher on the CEI Index (CEI Index, 2017).

In the UK, 66 percent of LGBT individuals have experienced a hate crime and reported it to no one (www.independent.co.uk, 2014). Only 6.3 percent of Chinese workers are completely out at work (*Beijing Today*, 5/24/13). In some of the most populous countries—China, India and Russia—propaganda laws limit freedom of expression and can result in political imprisonment. African and Middle Eastern countries generally have some of the most severe penalties for being gay, up to life imprisonment and, in severe cases of human rights abuses, the death penalty. On the global stage, seventy-six countries still imprison LGBTQ citizens for the crime of being queer, and thirteen states can impose the death penalty. In December 2011, Hillary Clinton famously declared "LGBT rights are human rights and human rights are LGBT rights" in a speech to the US Mission to the United Nations in Geneva, Switzerland. Support of LGBT rights in a declaration to the UN Human Rights Council has been signed by ninety-six member-states of the United Nations (2011). Fortunately, seventy-six countries offer non-discrimination protections for their LGBTQ citizens, forty-seven countries recognize same-sex unions, and twenty-seven countries allow joint adoption (The International Lesbian, Gay, Bisexual, Transgender and Intersex Association, June 2016).

Legalized same-sex marriage is linked to fewer youth suicide attempts, a striking finding since suicide, after fatal injuries and homicides, is the most frequent cause of death for US citizens between the ages of fifteen and twenty-four. LGBTQ youth attempt suicide at four times the rate of heterosexual teens. The data in this same-sex marriage study reflected thirty-two states that legalized same-sex marriage between 2004 and 2015 and fifteen that did not. The study concluded that legalizing same-sex marriage was related to a drop in suicide attempts, most likely related to a reduction in social stigma. This Harvard-Johns Hopkins Schools of Public Health study has the validity of self-reported data from 750,000 students over the course of more than a decade, 1999-2015 (*JAMA Pediatrics*, Feb. 20, 2017).

So while the world is growing more tolerant of LGBTQ artists, icons, and everyday heroes, LGBTQ youth around the world are hungry for positive, successful, life-affirming, openly queer role models. A full 42 percent do not feel accepted in the communities where they live in America, and 92 percent hear negative messages about being LGBT at school, on the Internet, and from peers ("Growing Up LGBT in America," based on 10,000+ survey participants, ages 13-17, HRC, 2014).

It is also true that you must keep yourself safe wherever you are; it may mean remaining circumspect or even closeted. Sometimes it means moving to another city or creating a family of choice if your family of origin rejects you. It sometimes even means leaving your home country.

This book serves as a beacon to LGBTQ individuals around the world, demonstrating in real-life stories how it's possible to live happy, fulfilling, open queer lives. Being queer does not condemn you to a life of misery or a life in the closet. You do not have to seek sex in the shadows of parks and bathrooms. You can be out and successful at work. You can be happily married and raise a family if you choose. And unlike most of the books out there, this one doesn't end with its subjects committing suicide, murder, or dying alone. And unlike most of the queer anthologies, this one is not confined to only the most educated and affluent in Western society.

On these pages, you'll find someone just like you. From China to England, from The Netherlands to New Zealand, from Uruguay to the Philippines, from Vietnam to Argentina, from Belgium to Russia, from Ireland to Canada, from big cities on the coasts of America to small towns in the heartland. The message in these pages echoes the bravery of one Irish author of the last century, Oscar Wilde: "Be yourself. Everyone else is already taken."

"Be yourself. Everyone else is already taken."

Oscar Wilde,
1854-1900

Artists

1. **Richard Blanco,** Cuban-American, Presidential Inaugural Award-Winning Poet

2. **Carolina De Robertis,** Uruguayan Award-Winning Novelist and Translator

3. **Emma Donoghue,** Award-Winning Irish-Canadian Novelist, Screenwriter, and Playwright, Academy Award nominated film, *Room*

4. **Sean Dorsey,** Award-Winning Transgender Dancer, Choreographer, and Producer

5. **Thea Farhadian,** Violinist, Electronic Music Composer, and Co-Founder of Armenian Film Festival

6. **Bill T. Jones,** Two-Time Tony Award Winning African-American Choreographer, *Spring Awakening* and *Fela!*, and Dancer

7. **Tony Kushner,** Tony and Pulitzer Prize Award-Winning Playwright, Lyricist, and Emmy Award-Winning Screenwriter, *Angels in America*

8. **Maarten Mourik,** Dutch Singer, Songwriter, Author, and Independent Theater and Film Director

9. **Laurie Rubin,** Blind Mezzo-Soprano, Author, and Lyricist; Co-Founder of Ohana Arts

10. **Colm Toibin,** Award-Winning Irish Novelist, Short-Listed for the Man Booker Prize Three Times, Author of Academy Award-nominated film, *Brooklyn*

Richard Blanco: Poet Exile

First Immigrant, Youngest and Only Gay Inaugural Poet, 2013

Award-Winning Cuban-American Poet
Paterson Poetry Prize and Thom Gunn Award for Poetry

"I think we're finally *Americanos*," Richard Blanco, Cuban immigrant poet, leaned over and whispered to his mother that cold January day in Washington, DC in 2013 when Barack Obama was sworn in to his second term as President of the United States. Blanco, only the fifth inauguration poet since Robert Frost during the Kennedy presidency, was the first immigrant, the first openly gay, and the youngest poet ever to read before a televised audience of 21.6 million viewers and more than a million Obama supporters present on the Washington Mall. Once known in Miami, Florida as the Poet Engineer, Blanco began his career as a civil engineer. Like many working class kids from immigrant families, Blanco was encouraged to graduate from Florida International University in engineering in 1991 and "get a good job." He came relatively late to poetry, began writing at age twenty-five, and graduated with an MFA in Creative Writing in 1997 from his alma mater at age twenty-nine. However, since that very public reading of his universal poem, "One Today," Blanco feels he's come to a fork in the road and that he will be writing for the rest of his life. Now forty-eight, Blanco was appointed by the Academy of American Poets as the first-ever Education Ambassador and meets with teachers, "turning people on to poetry."

In fact, in 2015, his poem, "One Today", was made into an illustrated children's book. "We didn't change a word," he said. In this poem, Blanco so eloquently lays out the American dream: "*One sun rose on us today* "*One light, waking up rooftops, under each one, a story/ "We head home: through the gloss of rain or weight/ of snow, or the plum blush of dusk, but always - home, / always under one sky, our sky. And always one moon...*"

Richard Blanco, winner of the 2013 Paterson Poetry Prize and the Thom Gunn Award for Poetry for his collection, *Looking for the Gulf Motel,* and the 2015 Lambda Literary Award for Best Gay Memoir, *The Prince of los Cocuyos,* has, by the very "act of being who I am," created a positive impression of gay people to the American public. Maybe because of his

"One Today" Inaugural poem presented to President Barack Obama.

Photo by Pete Souza

renewed their deeply abiding friendship, nurtured over the years—allies in the lexicon of Latino literature.

His favorite poet is Elizabeth Bishop. He was surprised to find himself in someone he didn't expect—not just who, but what and how she writes: complex, telling a story through rich

Richard Blanco (R) and partner of 15 years, Dr. Mark Neveu, on Glacier Hike in Iceland.

Photo by Pete Souza

imagery. Though a woman born in Worchester, MA, in a way she was an exile all her life, living in Canada, Brazil, and America. "I think I feel like an exile every day of my life. Many different layers—exile from myself, being who I am, separate from family. The world is becoming more fluid. Living in different cultures is the underlying universal story of me and my parents—exile. I've moved a lot. I feel very much like an immigrant - different foods, regional history, community. I'm always engaged in that space of the mind that seeks out the sense of home and identity," Blanco explained.

Blanco sees poetry as the bridge between people because, "no matter what culture we're from, we're all operating from the same set of core human emotional denominators— love, hate, betrayal, loss, grief, hurt, anger, redemption and reconciliation."

In fact, Blanco was commissioned to write a poem for the re-opening of the US Embassy in Cuba in August of 2015. He wrote a poem, entitled, "Cosas Del Mar" (Matters of the Sea): "The sea doesn't matter what matters is this: that we all belong to the sea between us "No one is other to the other to the sea." This poem begins to heal the rift bigger than the ninety miles of sea that separates Havana from Miami ever since the US severed diplomatic relations with Castro's Cuba in 1961.

Blanco crosses boundaries in his fundamental human drive for home, belonging, and becoming. Many have told him, including his Polish-German partner, Mark Neveu, of fifteen years, that the *abuela* in his memoir reminds them of their own grandmothers, their own families. It is this common humanity that enables Blanco to at least try to tap into something larger. "What is *West Side Story* if not *Romeo and Juliet* told all over again? Human motives and emotions represent the same universal element that we all share."

Blanco understands the practical constraints that everyone has; he does not view having a job as being a sellout. Most

Richard Blanco and Carole King at
Boston Strong Event.

Photo by Alissa Hessler

artists have to have another means of support to make a living. But he would advise, "Do not lose sight of what you want to do as an artist. Make decisions that support your ultimate goal; I turned down promotions so I could have energy for my work. Make life decisions, visioning your art and building your life around that. Most importantly, work. Work and keep on working. Art is not just something that happens; it's something you MAKE happen."

"Most importantly, work. Work and keep on working. Art is not just something that happens; it's something you MAKE happen."

Richard Blanco

Carolina De Robertis: From Uruguay with Love

Carolina De Robertis: From Uruguay with Love
Award-Winning Novelist: *Gods of Tango, Perla, The Invisible Mountain*

Best 10 Books for a First Novel by *Booklist*, Recipient of Italy's Regium Julii Prize

2012 National Endowment for the Arts fellowship
Translator, Faculty, MFA, Literary Translation, Creative Writing Department at
San Francisco State University

More than a courageous author, Carolina De Robertis has braved rejection from her Uruguayan family of origin. In 2002, when De Robertis married a woman, African-American filmmaker Pamela Harris, her parents cut her out of their lives. Becoming pregnant and bearing two children did not soften her parents in any way. "In fact, they dug their heels in even more. I suffered what Sarah Schulman has called, 'familial homophobia,' and had to mourn my parents, grieve the loss as though it were a death, though my parents are both alive." When her father's siblings tried to approach Carolina's father to encourage him to mend relations, he responded by cutting off contact with them.

De Robertis is of many countries, yet an outsider in all of them. Born in England in 1975 and raised in England, Switzerland and the US by Uruguayan parents, she always has an "insider-outsider perspective, a double lens, if you will." She identifies as queer—very much so, yet is also married with children which can be seen as ho-hum suburban, picking the kids up from school and taking them to Kung Fu.

A self-described bookworm, De Robertis always had her "nose in a book" all her life. "One of the ways I became a reader was in Switzerland, between the ages of five and ten, I was ostracized by classmates and teachers—so I devised a way to survive. Reading gave me a freedom and world expansion that never left me. I just love books. I love language. I love people. Novels—I'm fascinated by people and in love with humanity. I am a curious mix: I love to be alone in a room and love to go out in the world and talk, especially about books."

Carolina De Robertis is an international sensation. Bestselling author of three novels, *The Gods of Tango, Perla* and *The Invisible Mountain,* De Robertis has garnered praise from *Publishers Weekly, Kirkus Review, Library Journal, Booklist, O, The Oprah Magazine,* and the *Washington Post,* to name just a few. De Robertis' debut novel, *The Invisible Mountain,* was winner of the *San Francisco Chronicle's* Best Book of 2009, named one of the Best 10 Books for a First Novel by *Booklist,* and recipient of Italy's Regium Julii Prize and a 2012 National Endowment for the Arts fellowship. Her work has been translated into seventeen languages, and she has translated Alejandro Zambra's *Bonsai,* made into a feature film, and Roberto Ampuero's *The Neruda Case,* from Spanish to English. Junot Diaz calls De Robertis "an extraordinarily courageous writer who only gets better with every book."

She is working on a fourth novel, set in Uruguay. She keeps returning to the *Rio de la Plata,* that river plate that divides Argentina from Uruguay. Her grandmother was an Argentinian poet and her father an Argentinian scientist. Both migrated to Uruguay at various times for various reasons. Her first novel, *The Invisible Mountain,* traced three generations of Uruguayan women and built the story around a mystical myth of the appearance of purple berries at the altar of a church in 1800. It was a story of succulent and perfectly ripe berries, enough to feed the town twice over. The priest collapsed: "He just turned white, white as paper, then he went pink, and his eyes rolled into his head "he collapsed onto the ground "It was the smell that was too much for him. You know. Like the smell of a woman who's been satisfied. *El pobre padre.* All those nights alone - he couldn't take it, those berries hot from the sun, in his church,

too much for a priest."' De Robertis invokes the magical
realism of Gabriel Garcia Marquez and the poetic sensuality
of Pablo Neruda in one breath.

While *The Invisible Mountain* was very much a story
told in the magical realism of South America, *Perla*, De
Robertis' second novel, was told in the modern realistic
vein of transforming historical events into stories told by
pivotal characters. Perla, the son of a military leader who
orchestrated the *Desaparecidos, The Disappeared*, during
the dark years of Argentina's military dictatorship between
1976-1983, exposed by the mothers and grandmothers in
the Plaza de Mayo, is the story of discovery and anguish.
De Robertis writes, "Sometimes, to hide your sadness, you
have to cut yourself in two. That way you can bury half
of yourself, the unspeakable half, and leave the rest to face
to the world." She sometimes felt this way, especially in her
early twenties, when she was breaking away from her
parents, taking huge risks, in a lot of pain.

As for being in the closet, De Robertis has always felt "it's harder
to be *in* the closet, than *out* of the closet. In fact, it's intolerable to
live in the closet. To hide, being your full self. Not everyone has
a choice: they may not be safe out of the closet."

In *Perla*, De Robertis spares no one in her effort to make
beauty out of suffering. In life, in fact, De Robertis was a
rape counselor for ten years and heard more than 1,000
stories of trauma and suffering, but also heard of resilience
and triumph, an incredible part of the human story. It was
this human spirit revealed that allowed De Robertis to do
that work for so long.

In her third novel, *The Gods of Tango*, De Robertis evokes
the character of Leda, a seventeen-year-old immigrant
from a small village in Naples who arrives in Buenos
Aires in 1913, only to find that her cousin/fiancé, Dante, has
been murdered. Left to her own devices, at a time when
women survived as either seamstresses in sweat shops or as
prostitutes, Leda becomes Dante, a cross-dressing man. He
goes out at night with his grandfather's violin and joins a
Tango *orquesta*. Little did De Robertis realize more than five
years ago when she began writing *Gods of Tango* just how
topical the subject of cross-dressing and transgender would
become with the coming out of Caitlin Jenner.

De Robertis steams up the pages of her third novel with sex
scenes that are so intimate, so revealing:

She "let her hands and mouth lead the way, to the nape of
Alma's neck, the arms, breasts, waist and neither of them
made a sound just as two tango dancers move without a
word, shut up and let your body do the speaking like this,
this, this "she made sounds as though she were fighting
something back - a jaguar, a shark, a sword of joy. Then,
she lost the fight, and as sensation stabbed her Dante held
fast to Alma's hips to keep her own mouth fused in place as
she'd learned to do with *Mamita*, accompanying the storm,
swallowed by it, lit up in every centimeter of her body.

In describing her process, De Robertis said, "It was an
extraordinary risk to embark on this book, but once an idea
takes hold of me, I can't write anything else. I've learned
in fifteen years of novel writing - the voice of the book
that wants to be written through you; the sooner I can get

out of my way; move past fear, the better things go," De
Robertis said. In spite of the rather racy scene, it was not
scary to write; it was thrilling and exciting to write, rather,
as there is an incredible dearth of true real writing of sex
between women."

De Robertis gives voice to gender awakening when she
describes how Dante feels:

"Sometime in those years, the Shift occurred, though Dante
would never be sure of the exact moment, just as one can't
know precisely where the river ends and the great Atlantic
begins: but one day he simply knew it, simply found himself
as he, at home in the pronoun the world gave him each day,
not because his body had changed, not because his story had
changed, not even because he didn't see himself as a woman,
but simply because the gap between inside and outside, self
and disguise, truth and pretense, had narrowed and thinned
until it became invisible to the human eye."

To look at De Robertis, in her flowing long hair and big
jewelry, one would never think she could understand, let
alone embody, the male form. Yet in this daring novel,
through the metaphor of *Tango*, De Robertis sifts through the
mystery of gender and gives us the unforgettable character
of Dante.

Though she's paid a price for being openly queer, she
considers herself happily queer. Fortunately, De Robertis
has been able to forge relationships with her siblings, aunts,
uncles, and cousins in Uruguay, Argentina, and Italy. Now
her children have relatives all over South America and

Europe who are crazy about them. She lives in Oakland, California, a city with the highest concentration of lesbian couples, where it's easy to find a wide variety of LGBTQ activities, performances, families, and community.

If she were to give any advice to young queer people, it would be this: "Create your life. Ask yourself what true meaning and joy is for you. Find a way to shape yourself. Living queer - so many dazzling, marvelous ways queer people can fashion a marvelous life. Never lose sight of that."

"Create your life. Ask yourself what true meaning and joy is for you. Find a way to shape yourself. Living queer - so many dazzling, marvelous ways queer people can fashion a marvelous life. Never lose sight of that."

Carolina De Robertis

Emma Donoghue: Irish-Canadian Writer Meets Hollywood

Award-Winning Novelist and Screenwriter

Academy Award-Nominated Screenwriter and Canadian Screen
Award-Winning Screenwriter

For a "Dublin girl from peasant stock," Emma Donoghue made a surprising entrée into the Hollywood elite. She joined a group of veteran screenwriters as the nominee for Best Adapted Screenplay at the 88th 2016 Academy Awards, for her first feature-length screenplay, fashioned from her own best-selling novel, *Room*. While Donoghue did not win, her "Ma" character, Brie Larson, won for Best Actress and named Donoghue in her acceptance speech. A month later, Donoghue and the film, *Room*, were crowned with Canada's highest awards, nine in all, including Best Picture and Best Adapted Screenplay at the Canadian Screen Awards.

Monumental Pictures has optioned her eighth novel, *Frog Music,* set in 1870s San Francisco, and Donoghue is adapting the screenplay for this film.

Donoghue, ever the writer, published another novel in September of 2016, *The Wonder,* about a nineteenth-century Irish girl who claims not to eat. In a country where approximately a million people starved and a million more emigrated from Ireland during *Gorta Mór,* the Great Famine—sometimes known as the Irish Potato Famine from 1845-1852—this is another of those stories that has yet to be told from such a unique vantage point.

Donoghue made her living as a writer for the first twenty-five years of her writing career and became more high-profile after her 2016 Academy Award nomination and Canadian Screen Award. Her historical novels include: *The Sealed Letter, Life Mask,* and *Slammerkin,* set in eighteenth- and nineteenth-century Britain. Her contemporary novels—*Landing, Hood* and *Stir-fry*—feature lesbian characters at the center. She's written many plays and short story collections before achieving global best-seller status with *Room.* Emma Donoghue has this advice for writers: "My experience is a fluke. So don't delude yourself that it's the job that's thwarting your wish to write the great novel. Many great first or fifth or tenth novels are written by people with jobs who somehow—and they have all my respect—summon up the energy before or after work to write." Outside writing, the only job Emma ever had was as a summer chambermaid, from which she was fired. Born in 1969, success is lapping at her doorstep at her home in London, Ontario that she shares with Canadian French and

Women's Studies academic Christine Roulston and their two children, Finn (b. 2003) and Una (b. 2007).

When Donoghue was short-listed for the Man Booker Prize for her novel *Room*, she said she was able to "stride proudly to the bakery "If I hadn't been on the short list, I would have had to stay home this week, because I couldn't stand all the little nods of sympathy" (*The Globe and Mail*, 9/7/10). Ever self-effacing, she said she felt like a tourist on the runway of all the award shows honoring *Room*. She did wear a full-length gown, but aside from that, *haute couture* is not her thing. *Room* was Donoghue's first "high-concept" novel. She had a good feeling about it from the start and it wrote so easily.

Donoghue has managed to bring lesbians into the literary pantheon of good writing with her consummate storytelling skills. Her first novel, *Stir-fry*, written at age twenty-one, presaged her talent. "This evocative and insightful novel is destined to become a classic in lesbian literature," The *Village Voice* opined. Her second novel, *Hood*, re-released following her success with *Room*, encapsulates the singular season of grief in the container of a week. A closeted lesbian has lost her lover in a car accident and reckons with the loss alongside some unexpected companions. Pen is still in the closet, teaching at her old school, living under the roof of Cara's gentle father, who thinks of her as his daughter's friend. How can she survive widowhood without even daring to claim the word? *Hood* answers the question.

Donoghue was "tickled pink it's been re-released "I suppose *Hood*—being the first of my books that made me stretch into making-it-all-up territory—gave me confidence for other

challenges to come. You also take what you've lived and
extrapolate from it; I knew what it was like to be dumped
and figured bereavement would have at least something in
common with that."

Never in the margins or relegated to the LGBTQ sections
of bookstores, Donoghue tackles the tough subjects—love,
infidelity, mother-child bonds, family, class, immigration,
and death. Educated at University College, Dublin, and
the University of Cambridge, England, Donoghue, PhD,
writes with an unparalleled command of language and a
piercing understanding of the human heart. That is why
her strong voice has emerged above the din, catapulting
Donoghue, a lesbian writer, into the wide world of literary
and film achievement. "I think the most important way to
resist pigeonholing is to write about LGBTQ matters without
apology, but also without coziness—assuming an LGBTQ
readership—or crankiness—lecturing a straight readership. It
also helps if you concentrate on some big life-or-death topics
that matter to everybody. But you know, I've never objected
to being called a lesbian writer, that would be bad manners,
like badmouthing your own ethnic group," she said.

The Golden Box Office Award, given to a Canadian film by
a Canadian director/screenwriter that performs exceptionally
well at the box office, earning at least $1 million, comes
with a cash prize of $40,000, which is usually shared by
the director and screenwriter. Because *Room* director Lenny
Abrahamson is not Canadian, Donoghue won half the
award, $20,000, at the Canadian Screen Awards. However,
she decided to donate the money to the ImagineNATIVE
Film + Media Arts Festival, which features aboriginal

projects. "I think everyone can agree that this particular
year there's no doubt that how to make the film industry
better is to make it more diverse," said Donoghue. "And as a
woman entering into screenwriting, where we are probably
a minority compared with men, I'm so aware that you need
help to get into an industry that can seem like it has closed
walls" (*The Canadian Press*, 3/15/16).

What advice would Donoghue give to anyone who wants
to become a writer? "Write a lot, write with passion. Don't
give up the day job till you have reason to believe you can
live off your writing, because plenty of great books have
been written at weekends, and why put your art under
pressure to be profitable? If you write poems or stories,
submit them to magazines. If you write a novel, rewrite it
several times, and then, only when you think it's great, try
to find an agent who'll sell it to a publisher."

Critics have honored Donoghue with the highest praise in
a numbed social media-driven world: "Donoghue's great
strength—apart from her storytelling gift—is her emotional
intelligence" (*Irish Independent*, 2010). The BBC Radio Ulster
called her 2012 full-length play, *The Talk of the Town*,
"mesmerizing." The *NY Times* lauded *Room*: "This is a truly
memorable novel, one that can be read through myriad
lenses—psychological, sociological, political. It presents an
utterly unique way to talk about love, all the while giving
us a fresh, expansive eye on the world in which we live."

The most amazing thing about Emma Donoghue is how she
is responding to this new-found fame. Co-creating this indie
film with the Irish and Canadian Film Boards and working

closely with fellow Dubliner,
Director Lenny Abrahamson,
Donoghue holds no illusions about
the film's uncommon success.
She does hold to the truth of
her novel, an exploration of the
mother-child bond, written when
Donoghue was the mother of a
four-year-old boy and a one-
year-old girl. She considers *Room*
an extraordinary love story. As
for how this independent, small-
budget, nuanced film reached
such commercial heights against a
backdrop of big-budget films, she
reacts in a 2016 TVO interview
with Steve Paiken, "Who needs
'em—car chases, special effects—
they do not touch the heart."
That's why Donoghue kept the
rights to her novel and wrote
the screenplay herself. Her only
complaint now: "The perverse
thing about success—it leads to lots
of interviews."

"I think the most
important way to resist
pigeonholing is to write
about LGBTQ matters
without apology,
but also without
coziness—assuming an
LGBTQ readership—or
crankiness—lecturing
a straight readership.
It also helps if you
concentrate on some big
life-or-death topics that
matter to everybody.
But you know, I've never
objected to being called
a lesbian writer, that
would be bad manners,
like badmouthing your
own ethnic group."

Emma Donoghue

Sean Dorsey Breaks Ground: Transgender and Queer Choreographer and Dancer

Founder and Artistic Director, Fresh Meat Productions (2001-Present)
First Nonprofit in the US to create, present, and tour year-round multidisciplinary transgender arts programs
Produces annual Fresh Meat Festival of Transgender and Queer Performance each June

Artistic Director, Sean Dorsey Dance (2005-Present)
Four-Time Izzie (Isadora Duncan) Award-Winning Company

One of the world's first openly transgender professional choreographers and dancers creates powerful dances that combine full-throttle movement and storytelling to bring transgender and queer stories to the stage. Sean Dorsey has won four Isadora Duncan Dance Awards (Izzies)—the San Francisco Modern Dance equivalent of the Academy Awards.

Sean Dorsey gives voice to longtime survivors of the early AIDS epidemic in his award-winning work *THE MISSING GENERATION*—which he created after traveling the US for two years to record oral histories with LGBT longtime survivors. Dorsey reminds audiences of the homophobia, transphobia, secrecy, police brutality, and discrimination trans and queer people experienced decades ago—but also how they found love and community—in *The Secret History of Love*, the result of his oral history interviews with LGBT elders.

But Dorsey came to dance late. He took hobby courses, a summer jazz workshop, jazz and modern dance classes at the University of British Columbia, while studying political science and Women's Studies. "Before that point, I'd never seen anybody like me in dance. When I was in high school, there was no Gay-Straight Alliance. There was nobody who was out in my high school as queer or trans, so it was unthinkable that somebody like me would be in dance, let alone in choreography. It wasn't until these hobby classes I took during grad school when ballet and modern dance professional teachers suggested to me that I could be a professional dancer that the possibility even entered my mind," said Dorsey.

Sean is from Vancouver, Canada, and his mother is a feminist and lesbian. His mom was a very out feminist. So, Sean grew up with a fire for social justice; in high school, he was given an award for social responsibility because of his activism as a teen. When Sean came out, all his family was very loving and supportive. While he was afraid to tell one grandmother and a great aunt in their early 90s, both separately said something like, "Oh, honey, I always knew you were trans. I was just waiting for you to feel comfortable enough to let me know. I love you very much."

After immersing himself in professional dance training at age twenty-five for two years, dancing for eight hours a day at a dance school called Main Dance in Vancouver, Sean came to the San Francisco Bay Area in 2001, founded Fresh Meat Productions and the Fresh Meat Festival in 2002, and Sean Dorsey Dance in 2005. He also danced with Lizz Roman and Dancers, a daring site-specific dance company, for six years.

"Every transgender person has a unique journey. Most of us have stories that don't fit the mainstream 'I was born in the wrong body' narrative. Generally, it's not our own feelings about our trans bodies and identities that cause us the most pain—it's the discomfort and discrimination we endure from the rest of the world! I was out for seven or eight years as transgender before I had chest surgery, and for ten years before I chose to take hormones. I danced professionally with Lizz Roman and other companies and was out as trans. Because I chose not to take testosterone, for ten years I didn't have the low voice I have now, so I wasn't always read by the world as male and was often mis-gendered—which is painful."

"The hardest part of being a trans dancer is not having peers or mentors. Simple things like walking into a new dance studio, going into gendered bathrooms, using a gendered changing room and changing clothes before class are very difficult. Modern dance is a profoundly gendered field and very few people have done the work necessary to make their studios, companies or theaters welcoming or safe for trans people. This is part of the work I do now on tour, teaching classes and workshops across the country—creating safe dancing spaces for trans and gender non-conforming people," said Sean.

Sean Dorsey is the Artistic Director and choreographer of Sean Dorsey Dance (he also performs in his work) and the Artistic Director of Fresh Meat Productions, one of the first year-round transgender multidisciplinary arts nonprofit organizations in the world. In 2012, Fresh Meat Productions became the first transgender organization to be awarded a National Endowment for the Arts grant.

Sean Dorsey is young, but is well aware of the groundbreaking and heartbreaking work that his LGBTQ elders and ancestors have done before him: "This is what drives me as an artist and an activist: our trans and queer stories aren't recorded in mainstream history—and are often left out of the family album. My work as a trans artist is to bring our stories to light—in a way that is accessible and resonant for trans, queer and straight audiences alike. This is why I recorded oral histories with trans and queer elders to create my last two productions, *THE MISSING GENERATION* (currently on a 20-city tour of the U.S.) and

The Secret History of Love (which recently completed a 20-city tour)."

 At performances of *THE MISSING GENERATION*, sold-out audiences of young and old, straight and queer, dancer and non-dancer, sit next to one another in the theater, tears

Sean Dorsey and Shawna Virago.

Photo by Lydia Daniller

rolling down their faces. For those caregivers, survivors who escaped AIDS, and longtime survivors living with HIV/ AIDS, *THE MISSING GENERATION* is a powerful reminder of the losses of the '80s and '90s of so many gay, bi, and trans people to AIDS, as well as a testament to the beauty and power of the communities who held those losses and fought for justice.

The Secret History of Love reveals the underground ways that trans and queer people managed to find love and community in decades past when it was illegal to gather in public or wear clothing of the "opposite" gender. The show's sound score includes excerpts from the oral history interviews, including bold declarations of love in the face of great danger for those open queers and trans people in the '50s and '60s. Before STONEWALL, LGBTQ people could be fired, exposed, beat up or even murdered without any rights, protections or recourse. Lesbians, gays, and trans people could lose their children and their families of origin. Financial and emotional ruin was and still is, especially for trans people, a very real possibility in America.

Dorsey feels strongly that the queer community needs to remember and know the stories of the past. His work attracts intergenerational audiences and opens up the conversation between trans and queer, queer and straight, old and young. That dialogue moves hearts and minds. Every Sean Dorsey Dance performance spills over into the lobby for wine, non-alcoholic beverages and conversations to continue. "I'm always mindful of how my elders and ancestors' art and activism and struggles made my life possible" Dorsey said.

Fresh Meat Festival, produced by Fresh Meat Productions, is not a low-quality community performing arts program. It's a professionally staged and well-curated set of performances by diverse artists. Professional ballroom dance champions; original music; spoken word; performance art; comedy; Taiko drumming; all this and more is found at the festival. The eclectic festival, produced annually during Pride month, is ever-changing, with eternally strong production values. Fifteen years after founding Fresh Meat Productions, Dorsey continues to curate and produce the sold-out performances.

In an increasingly gentrified San Francisco, Sean and his partner of fifteen years, fellow transgender activist, musician, and singer-songwriter Shawna Virago, live in the same rent-controlled house Shawna's lived in for twenty years. "We have a truly lovely, wonderful, kind landlord who's very generous. He loves us and we love him. That's a big reason we can be here making work in San Francisco. My work with my dance company, Sean Dorsey Dance, and Fresh Meat Productions allow me to sustain myself as an artist. We are always busy because we operate year-round programs—making new work, the Festival in June, the Sean Dorsey Dance home season in April, the Sean Dorsey Dance year-round national touring, and LGBT-friendly dance and self-expression workshops across the US."

Sean considers himself foremost a choreographer and dancer—but always an activist. It is that passion that led him to leap onto the stage as an openly transgender modern dancer and choreographer: to make dances, but also to work for justice.

Transgender people still face legally-codified and socially-sanctioned discrimination in the nation and the state's criminal justice, employment, education, and healthcare systems. Trans people experience a disproportionate percentage of hate crimes and police brutality—90 percent have experienced harassment on the job; 61 percent have experienced physical assault; 64 percent have experienced sexual assault; transgender households are four times more likely to have an annual household income below $10,000 compared to the cisgender population; and 47 percent have been fired for being transgender (National Center for Transgender Equality, National Gay and Lesbian Task Force, GLAAD, 2013-15). Added to this, transgender people rarely see affirmative representations of themselves in dance, the performing arts, or the media.

Dorsey's advice to any transgender person who wants to become a professional dancer is: "GO FOR IT! I want to see transgender dancers feel empowered and beautiful in their bodies and feel that dancing is our birthright. Make sure you're connected to support during training rehearsals and time spent in the field. As trans people, using our bodies as our primary instrument in a highly-gendered field, hard stuff can come up—either feelings you have about your body or feelings or judgments other people have about your body. There is so much gender-based casting, gendered roles and gendered partnering in dance—this is painful." Sean encourages everyone to "adopt some kind of *self-kindness* practice. One thing anyone can do is put a hand over your heart and give yourself positive messages. You can look in the mirror and tell yourself that your body is beautiful. All people, especially trans people and queer people, people from communities of

color and people with disabilities
have wounded hearts and feelings
because we have been given
so many negative and hateful
messages from other people about
our bodies—we can really benefit
from a *self-kindness* practice."

Brain science now proves
that affirmations, whether or
not consciously believed, can
actually rewire hardwired
neural pathways, laying down
new tracks in the brain, carving
grooves, expanding dendrites
and firing synapses, changing
brain chemistry and brain
circuitry ("Brain Scans Can Help
Explain Why Self-Affirmation
Works," Christian Jarrett, *New
York Magazine*, 11/16/15).
For trans people who suffer
disproportionately from bias, these
emerging findings offer hope.

For Sean Dorsey, who lives on
more than hope, life is good. At
forty-four, in a long-term happy
relationship for fifteen years with
a transwoman artist, doing work
he loves in a city that protects and
supports trans people and loves the

"GO FOR IT! I want to
see transgender dancers
feel empowered and
beautiful in their bodies
and feel that dancing
is our birthright. Make
sure you're connected to
support during training
rehearsals and time
spent in the field."

Sean Dorsey

arts, he has defied the statistics. A professional choreographer and dancer for nearly twenty years, founding director of the nation's first year-round transgender multidisciplinary arts nonprofit for fifteen years: Sean is ready for the next artistic mountain to climb.

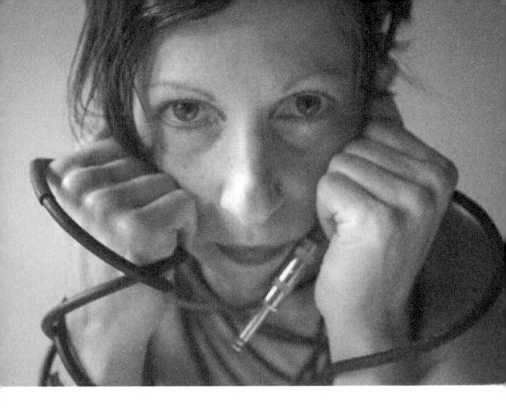

Thea Farhadian: Variations on a Theme

Composer and Professional Violinist, formerly under Conductor
Kent Nagano

Co-Founder of the Armenian Film Festival, NYC and San
Francisco

When she was a child, she wanted to be a rock star. At age four, she wanted to play the violin because she thought it was a guitar. By age six, Thea Farhadian was taking violin lessons from some of the top music teachers, including Gerard Svazlian, in the San Francisco Bay Area. Trained as a classical violinist, Thea defied her parents' more practical expectations and became a professional violinist with the Berkeley Symphony under Conductor Kent Nagano, now conductor of the Orchestre Symphonique Montreal. "It was an honor to play under him," Thea said.

Thea's parents loved music, but expected that their oldest daughter would pursue something more practical as a career. She realized much later that her parents were children the Depression, which affected their views on the place music should play in one's life. Though her father was an accomplished violist with a budding talent aborted by a World War II injury, her aunt a classical pianist, curtailed by lack of support, and her grandfather a kanun player, composing in the Armenian style, music was all around her, but never viewed as a viable profession. This made pursuing music in such a singular way a challenge for Thea at times.

If the clock were thirty hours instead of twenty-four, Farhadian would have remained with the Berkeley Symphony under Kent Nagano. She loved the orchestra and the contemporary classical music Nagano brought to the intellectual audiences in Berkeley. However, Thea was called to create, and after ten years as a classical freelancer, she found her composing interest and allied with two San Francisco Bay Area groups, *Composers Cafeteria* and *Ovaryaction*. They played and performed one another's compositions. "I found my own voice through improvising and working with others," she said.

A third-generation Armenian-American, Thea is the granddaughter of Valentine Babagian, who survived the Armenian Genocide of 1915. Her grandmother escaped Eastern Turkey and the Genocide as a nine-year-old stowaway on a ship to America. She accompanied her mother and sister after losing her father and brother in the genocide. The family only had money for two tickets. In spite of her trauma, which she spoke little about, Thea's grandmother did say, "There were some good Turks. Many tried to help us."

While Thea is several generations removed from the catastrophe, her Armenian roots propelled her to curate, along with Anahid Kassabian, the Armenian Film Festival, first launched at the Cantor Film Center on the New York University campus in 2002. Farhadian, Kassabian and Hrayr Eulmessekian co-curated the Armenian Film Festival in San Francisco in 2004 and 2006. Not wanting to deliver a genocide-only film festival, the three brought in contemporary Armenian films by and about Armenians, including biographies, features, documentaries, and shorts about everything from feminism to disability, from racism to gender bending. Their goal was to reach Armenian and general audiences and present the complexity in contemporary Armenian life from Armenia and the Diaspora.

Following a master's degree in interdisciplinary arts at San Francisco State University, Farhadian taught violin in public schools for the next ten years. Drawn to other styles, she studied Arabic classical music in Cairo with Alfred Gamil, Georges Lamman in San Francisco, and Simon Shaheen in New York City. In 2007, she completed an MFA in Electronic Music at Mills College in Oakland, and was influenced by electronic and improvised music mavericks Maggi Payne, John Bishoff, Chris Brown, and Fred Frith, pioneers in electronic music and recording.

She's performed solo electronics in Berkeley, Berlin, Italy, New York, and San Francisco, and sound art in Armenia, Scotland, Switzerland, and Yemen. With residencies in Amman, Jordan, and Amsterdam, The Netherlands, Farhadian expanded her sound composition repertoire. Given an artist-in-residency appointment at Villa Montalvo in Saratoga, CA, Farhadian developed the work on her first solo electronic music composition release, *Tectonic Shifts*, from the Creative Sources Recordings label, launched at the San Francisco Electronic Music Festival in 2016 to rave reviews. One reviewer, Gino Robair, in *Electronic Musician*, said, "Real-time computer processing and improvisation are a tricky combination, but violinist Thea Farhadian handles both with exceptional skill and musicality "Farhadian uses Max/MSP to extend her instrument's timbral and rhythmic palette. "Simultaneously challenging and beautiful." *Textura* calls Thea Farhadian "an innovative violinist, composer, improviser, label founder and educator with home bases in San Francisco and Berlin. She's covered an incredible amount of ground in her life," and Rebecca Wishnia of the *San Francisco Classical Voice* calls Farhadian's sounds "lyrical and haunting." Her 2015 recordings *RedBlue* (with guitarist Dean Santomieri) and *eXcavations* (with double bassist Klaus Kürvers), were issued by BlackCopper Editions, a label she founded dedicated to improvised and experimental music.

Listening to Farhadian's violin with found objects, like rolled-up tinfoil processed through a synthesizer, at the annual New Music Bay Area Solstice Concert, Chapel of the Chimes

Thea Farhadian on violin.

Photo by Charles Armirkhanian, Other Minds

Mausoleum and Columbarium (designed by Julia Morgan), reminds one of the bold sounds John Cage created in the 1960s. "Musicians attaching objects to instruments to create a different sound started in the 1960s and opens up and expands the vocabulary of contemporary music. It comes from a tradition of experimentation. I would characterize my music as primarily abstract, very sound-based material that integrates tonality and micro tonality," Farhadian said.

Farhadian hasn't always wanted to compose. Trained in classical music, she was taught to be a performer, and that performers and composers are really separate. The old view of composition—writing notes on a staff of music—did not resonate with Thea. As a composer/improviser, starting with the Mills College community, she "improvised and composed at the same time. In some sense, you embrace everything you know and abandon everything you know at the same time. This mode resonates for me. I enjoy working with colleagues who work this way," she explained.

Not confined to the strict definition of music, Farhadian has explored the world of sound in her audio piece, *Voices Behind the Veil*, based on interviews with five Muslim women in Egypt—from unveiled to hijab-wearing, to full-veil-niqab-wearing fervent Muslims. Farhadian wanted to subvert the Western gaze and present Muslim women's views of wearing the veil or not wearing the veil from their own points of view. Set against the soundscape of Cairo street noises and the voices of the Muslim women in Arabic and English, the piece is designed to explode Western myths of veiling.

Working in collaboration is one of the ways Farhadian transcends the solo nature of performance. In her duets, she is both composing and improvising on the fly. There's a shared musical space. Farhadian, formerly a classical musician, and Santomieri, formerly a rock musician, work with both structured and free improvisations. With *eXcavations,*

Thea Farhadian and Dean Santomieri.

Photo by Viola Wu

double bassist Klaus Kürvers and violinist Thea Farhadian integrate raw string sounds with a rusty character. The result sounds both old and new. A poetic archiving, in a way.

Farhadian's music path has not come without obstacles. The hardest time in her personal history came when she was in a relationship with a female partner from another country. Most of her family did not accept Thea's partner. Her father, ill with cancer at the time, was the most kind and accepting, and that meant a lot to Thea. Much later on, her mother came to respect Thea's life choices. "In the end, I think having experienced being an outsider makes me much more empathetic to people regardless of their backgrounds or experiences," she said.

First and foremost, Thea Farhadian is an artist. She's paid the price and "wants to be seen for who I am and for my work to be heard and appreciated for what it is without my sexuality contextualizing it.

"I do like the term *queer* as it is a word chosen by a younger generation and it takes what was originally a negative term and transforms it." Her advice to young queer artists and musicians: "*Don't give up!*"

Thea Farhadian

That said, I do like the term *queer* as it is a word chosen by a younger generation and it takes what was originally a negative term and transforms it."

Her advice to young queer artists and musicians: "Don't give up!"

Bill T. Jones: Choreographer on the Cultural Forefront

Two-Time Tony Award-Winning Choreographer
MacArthur "Genius"

National Medal of Arts Winner

Bill T. Jones, two-time Tony Award-winning choreographer, MacArthur "Genius," National Medal of Arts and Doris Duke Artist Award-winner, crosses barriers to create works that tackle the *BIG* subjects: love, loneliness, identity, marginalization, loss of control, meaning, illness, death, and spiritual triumph. Jones is fearless while being afraid. "I think

Bill T. Jones and Bjorn Amelan, together since first
meeting in Paris, Feb. 16, 1992
Partners and arts collaborators
Bjorn Amelan is a set designer for NY LiveArts
Elisa Rolle, LiveJournal

it takes courage to be alive as a sensitive person, particularly in mid-life if you've been a performer as I have where your body is your stock and trade, your calling card and then your body is changing "It's a crap shoot. It's a beautiful crap shoot. But, it's a crap shoot," he said.

Jones was not always a dancer. He began life in 1952 in Bunnell, Florida, the tenth of twelve children born to migrant potato pickers who moved permanently to upstate New York, where Bill spent the bulk of his childhood. A theater major on an athletic scholarship to State University of New York in Binghamton, he found his calling when he wandered into an African dance class. The smell of sweat and dynamic pounding on the floor captivated him. Soon, he was eschewing track practice to take dance classes. There he met Arnie Zane, a Jewish-Italian white gay man, a SUNY graduate returning to study photography, who ventured into dance classes with Bill. That began a seventeen-year life and avant-garde modern dance partnership that ended with Zane's death at age thirty-nine as a result of AIDS.

The boundary-crossing work begun with the Bill T. Jones/ Arnie Zane Dance Company continues to this day with Jones' world premiere, *Analogy/Dora: Tramontane*. For this work, Jones drew upon ten years of interviewing Holocaust survivor Dora Amelan, the mother of his husband and life partner of twenty-four years, Bjorn Amelan, a Jewish French-Israeli sculptor and set designer. The new work depicts one refugee's journey in the midst of crisis. "Dora Amelan is a family member whom I love, not a newspaper article "Her experience opened history to me in a way the media cannot," Jones explained. That experience opens audiences and dance companies alike to the theme of Holocaust, not as an historical footnote, but as a very real and ongoing human crisis.

Still/Here remains one of the most controversial dance works created by Jones. He used his own experience of living with HIV since his diagnosis in 1986, and gathered non-dancers from around the country, working with them to express their feelings about living with life-threatening illness. He used that material—actual non-dancers and their stories—to meld with his dance company to create a dramatic paean to life. *Still* represented the quiet moment in response to diagnosis, and *Here* represented the dramatic sense of being present in the moment that often comes with the urgency of being told one has a life-threatening illness. Jones courageously told the untold stories of the many nameless life-threateningly ill around the country in a way that connected audiences to their own mortality, and stirred such controversy that one New York critic panned the work without even seeing it. It led to deeper questions: "What is the meaning of life? What brings meaning to your life? What do you love? Now, go do that."

Some of Jones' most emblematic works have occurred off Broadway. When Arnie Zane died, Jones danced *Absence* (1989), one of the most exquisite expressions of love and loss ever to grace the stage. Aged thirty-seven, he danced a duet with his now invisible partner, expressing in movement the inexpressible. "It was a gift actually. *Absence* connected me to the big spiritual existential questions about the nature of death, about love," Jones said.

However, the Broadway stage is where Bill T. Jones has garnered his widest audience. In 2007, he won the Tony Award for Best Choreography for the musical *Spring Awakening*, the story of a nineteenth-century German schoolgirl coming of age and the collective rebellion of German teens in an era of repression and structure. In *The Bitch of*

Bjorn Amelan and Bill T. Jones, Aberdeen Restaurant, White Plains, NY.

Photo by Chester Higgins Jr., NY Times

Living number shown at the 2007 Tony Awards, worldwide television audiences got to see the genius of Jones. He took schoolboy adolescents in laced up boots and uniforms and created a dance where they stomp and yell and break out of the strictures of their constrained upbringing. How did Jones relate to a culture so different from his own? "I didn't have to go back to the nineteenth century. Right, I'm a stomper, if that's what you mean...I think the Coming of Age story is told again and again in popular media "I did it with gestures and they turned out to be pretty universal, actually."

In 2010, American audiences saw and could begin to understand the experiences of African musicians and activists by looking at the world through Fela Kuti's eyes. Jones again succeeded in transporting mostly white middle class American audiences to conservative, corrupt Nigeria to meet *Fela!*, the Afrobeat musician and activist who was jailed nearly 200 times in his young life and had nearly every bone in his body broken by a repressive military regime. The thunder and pulse of Jones' second Tony Award-winning musical pushed audiences to stand up in the middle of the production and move their hips to Fela's "The Clock," adapted from Fela Kuti's stage performances. "There is a revolt in the way one lives in one's body and dancing in public, making yourself vulnerable to be looked at, to be seen" is revolutionary, Jones explained. This short scene in the musical has disrupted the theater experience forever. And, as Bill says, "the theater needs to be disrupted."

Exposing his own vulnerability is what endears Bill T. Jones to his young dancers, fellow choreographers, and wide audiences. Jones is seizing new opportunities to disseminate the language of the body even as his body ages, even as he is surrounded by the speedy, lithe, flexible pantheon of young dancers in his company. In 2011, Jones took on the great challenge of merging a dance company, the Bill T. Jones/Arnie Zane Dance Company, and a dance movement incubator space, the Dance Theater Workshop of New York,

Bill T. Jones receives the 2013 National Medal of Arts from President Barack Obama.

Photo by Pete Souza

to create an entirely new body arts organization, the New York Live Arts nonprofit, set in the heart of Chelsea. The unprecedented collaboration that created NY Live Arts, a service organization, has an Artistic Director who is a working choreographer with a resident company. Is Jones afraid of the responsibility as Cofounder and Artistic Director, of filling the 20,000-square foot home that houses a 184-seat theater and two 1,200-square foot studio spaces? You bet he is, but that has never stopped him from proceeding to create a place where "thinking and movement meet the future."

Determined to expose a broader range of audiences, particularly people of color, Jones has always been a "Black male in the white avant-garde his whole career. Don't get me wrong: I run a theater. How do we keep all the critics of the *NY Times* and middle class audiences happy and, at the same time, get people in there who want to bop along to *Hamilton?*...People who look very different than what we're up against in the downtown New York City art world "This country is so craven and profit-driven that when true art does not have a market value, people shun it. Every one of us whom I call cultural workers—how do we get the attention of an ever more attention-deficit population? I hope audiences will come closer to their own processes and realize they're collaborators in all cultural events, particularly in the theater. They are expected to be alive and very much aware of the myriad of things occurring on stage and the myriad of things occurring inside of themselves."

How does he work with NY Live Arts set designer and husband, Bjorn Amelan, and then go back home to Valley Cottage without feeling compressed? "Arnie Zane and I

built the dance company and
he and I were companions for
seventeen years until he died. I've
never done it any other way. I
can't even imagine a relationship
where you go home and where
you talk about your work that
day at the stock market and I
talk about my work that day at
the studio "I don't think that the
separation between life and art
exists in that way."

Analogy/ Dora: Tramontane is
Jones' latest work and is part of
a trilogy. Part II, *Analogy/Lance:
Pretty aka The Escape Artist* and
Part III, *Analogy/ Ambrose: The
Emigrant* will be performed in
2016 and 2017. The third work
uses the German novel, *The
Emigrants* by W.G. Sebald, as
its point of departure. Jones will
continue to perform *Story/Time*,
inspired by John Cage's 1959
Indeterminacy, a compendium
of 180 one-minute everyday Bill
T. Jones stories, seventy of which
are recited on stage with young
dancers swirling all around him.

"This country is so
craven and profit-
driven that when true
art does not have a
market value, people
shun it. Every one of
us whom I call cultural
workers—how do we get
the attention of an ever
more attention-deficit
population? "

Bill T. Jones

The best advice that guides him today came early on from his mother, who had seen "a vale of sorrows" and said to him, "Life ain't nothin' child than putting one foot in front of another." Bill T. Jones has done just that and more in his creative life.

Ph: Joan Marcus

Tony Kushner: An Angel in America

Tony Award and Pulitzer Prize-Winning Playwright

Emmy Award-Winning Screenwriter

Trudging across the marshy fields of Lake Charles, Louisiana, the slight adolescent was carrying a heavy wooden case that housed his cello. He slipped in the mud and his case broke open, sending the bridge, finger board and peg box flying. When he got to his father's university office and told him the story, his father said, "You don't really like this and I don't think you should play anymore. I don't want you to be part of the orchestra." His father had taken over the Governor's Program for Gifted Children as orchestra conductor for his very sick mother. Tony reacted, "Good. I don't want to be in your orchestra. You're mean."

Tony Kushner and his father had a strained relationship when he was growing up. Tony believes his father realized he was gay as early as age two or three and he didn't like it—he didn't like Tony being called a sissy and didn't like Tony's lack of athletic ability and interest in sports. Tony was not alone in not fitting into the family dream. His older sister was born deaf in a family of professional musicians. William Kushner was a conductor and clarinetist, and Sylvia Kushner was an accomplished bassoonist. When Leslie Kushner was small, 1950s doctors blamed Tony's mother's professional gigs away from home for Leslie's "psychosomatic deafness." Doctors and psychologists insisted that mothers should not work and should stay at home. In denial, Tony's parents did not fit Leslie with hearing aids until she was four.

So, when Tony finally came out in his early twenties, it was his brilliant painter sister whom he first told. Both she and he shared outsider status in the family. Tony's younger brother,

Eric, is a principal hornist for the Vienna Philharmonic, so carried on the family's musical tradition.

Tony Kushner's mother and his father were working musicians. Born in Manhattan, New York City, they harbored concerns that their professional musician status and travel schedule would be too financially and emotionally costly to raise a family. Shortly after Tony's birth, they returned to Lake Charles, Louisiana, at the urging of Tony's grandfather, owner of a lumber business. They soon found their way back to professional musicianship and gave Tony Kushner a blueprint for living as a working artist.

William Kushner's two great loves were music and literature. He could quote Keats and Shakespeare by heart. So, Tony grew up hearing the words of the great literary giants in his own home.

Tony Kushner always wanted to be a working artist, though he never imagined his second play, *Angels in America*, would catapult him to fame and fortune. In the two-part play, *Angels in America: Millennium Approaches* and *Angels in America: Perestroika*, Kushner broke both the rules of play-making, staging a seven-hour epic over the course of two days, and the silence surrounding the AIDS epidemic in America. "In a sense, until *Hamilton* came along, nothing else since *Angels* has had that kind of impact. So most of what has happened to me as a professional writer is in one way or another traceable to *Angels in America*. The sweep of it would make a claim on the importance of gay people in American life. It presented the idea that what was happening in the lives of gay men and lesbians was a worthy subject for a really sprawling momentous play not only for the LGBTQ, but the American, community at large," Kushner said.

When *Angels* opened, it was a huge sensation in 1990, but Tony's mother never fully realized Kushner's success. She died at age sixty-seven of breast cancer in that same year. Tony was just thirty-four.

Tony Kushner's father was one of the first to read a draft of *Angels in America.* He called Tony and said, "I will tell you that I find some of this ugly in terms of the subject matter. I have a great deal of difficulty with it, but as writing, it's very beautiful and I think it's going to be a very big deal." Oskar Eustis at the Eureka Theater in San Francisco suggested the standard 2.5 hours as a guideline for the play's length. Eustis, now Artistic Director of the Public Theater of New York City and creative collaborator on the musical *Hamilton,* trusted Kushner's instincts, however.

Those instincts proved prescient. For the play, Tony Kushner won an unprecedented 1993 Tony Award and Pulitzer Prize for *Angels in America: Millennium Approaches* and a 1994 Tony Award for *Angels in America: Perestroika.* Kushner adapted the screenplay for the 2003 HBO Special, starring Meryl Streep, Mary Louise-Parker, Emma Thompson, and Al Pacino, which launched him on his screenwriting career.

As to the life of a working artist, Kushner says that "the play (*Angels*) certainly was my second play and it made me fairly well-known and gave me financial security, not a lifelong financial security, but certainly several years. It paid the bills and made it possible for me to do the kind of work I wanted to do without worrying too much about how to pay the rent. It established me as a playwright."

It was the HBO feature film that got the attention of film director Steven Spielberg. This led to Spielberg and

Mark Harris, Tony's husband, partners for 18 years, and Tony Kushner. broadway.com

Kushner's collaboration on a number of award-winning films, including *Munich,* starring Eric Bana and Daniel Craig, and *Lincoln,* starring Daniel Day-Lewis and Sally Field. He penned the adaptation of August Wilson's *Fences,* starring Denzel Washington and Viola Davis.

Tony Kushner, for all his achievements as an American playwright and screenwriter, remains not only modest, but assiduous in pursuit of his art. Seven years is not an uncommon length of time for Kushner to bring a play to the stage as he has done with his 2016 play, *The Intelligent Homosexual's Guide to Capitalism and Socialism with a Key to the Scriptures,* or *iHo.* The play opened at the 174-seat Hampstead Theater in London to stunning reviews: "Tony Kushner's new play becomes one of the most absorbing dramas on the London stage "*iHo* is a giant, fiercely argued investigation of American family life and leftwing politics. The title tips its hat to Bernard Shaw "" (Susannah Clapp, *The Guardian,* 10/30/16).

Like all protean artists, Kushner does not confine himself to dramatic theater, but has created an award-winning musical, *Caroline, or Change,* in collaboration with 2015 *Fun Home* Tony Award-winning composer, Jeanine Tesori. Of the *Fun Home* Tony Award, Kushner says, "I'm completely thrilled they won. They totally deserved it and it was a great musical "In every profession, there is gender bias, misogyny and sexism. It actually does grotesque things to humans. I fully believe if women were in positions of power in the Church, the pedophile scandal wouldn't have happened. I think if women were dominant in the US Congress things would actually get done. It's infuriating to me that during the Tony Award ceremony, when Lisa Kron, a lesbian, *Fun Home* Book and Lyrics, and Jeanine Tesori, straight, Composer, won for Best Musical, Best Book and Best Original Score, an historical moment, their acceptance speech was filmed off camera." Kushner wrote the book and lyrics while Tesori composed the music for *Caroline, or Change,* a musical that captured all the tension of a racially divided South in one pivotal moment of interaction between a character very much like Tony as a boy and a Black maid, very much like his maid, where she takes the change from the boy's pockets, as agreed to by the parents, and a row ensues. During the argument, the maid slays the boy with the comment, "We're not friends." The musical won Best Musical at the Olivier Awards for excellence in professional theatre in London in 2007. Many theatergoers mistook the relationship and told Tony, "I had a Black nanny, just like you." More heartening were the comments by young Blacks from the South who thanked Kushner for putting their mothers, often maids, front and center in a musical, where the main character is a "colored woman."

Tony Kushner, never one to shy away from controversy, caused a stir when he adapted the screenplay for the film *Munich,* a story of Israeli revenge in the aftermath of the Munich massacre at the 1972 Olympics by a Palestinian terrorist group, Black September. Honorary degrees were awarded and pulled and awarded again by Northeastern universities. Yet, Kushner donated $100,000 to his alma mater, Columbia University, where he studied Medieval Studies.

While at the Tisch School of the Arts, New York University for his graduate degree, Tony Kushner directed several plays, setting the stage for his life as a playwright.

Angels in America, the timeless story of the closet, AIDS, friendship, betrayal, love and loss, will be brought to the National Theater of London in May of 2017, expanding the audience for the play, as the National Theater is subsidized by the government, allowing greater access and ticket affordability.

His father, William Kushner, conductor of the Lake Charles Symphony for forty years, would die nineteen years after Kushner won his first Tony Award in 1993, in 2012. That gave Kushner and his father a long period to come to terms with each other, and they really did. Tony loved his father very much. At Kushner's commitment ceremony in New York, his father recited from memory Shakespeare's sonnet, "Let me not the marriage of true minds admit impediments." On William Kushner's tombstone are the words from Keats' *Ode to a Nightingale* he oft quoted: "Was it a vision, or a waking dream? / Fled is that music:—Do I wake or sleep?"

Kushner is working on a new film, in the grand tradition of feature films, about a pivotal moment in the life of Barbara Jordan, the first African-American Congresswoman to come from the Deep South, to be played by Viola Davis. Few know that Jordan suffered from multiple sclerosis and left politics at the peak of her career to pursue a career in academia. The crisis for the Lyndon Baines Johnson protégé? Yet to be revealed.

Though Tony Kushner is a private person, when the *NY Times* called him and his future husband, Mark Harris, an editor-at-large for *Entertainment Weekly*, to be the first gay couple featured in a separate Vows Column next to the Marriage Announcements, they agreed to it immediately: "We're both political people and we both take the struggle for LGBTQ rights seriously and we thought that something good can come out of it for our community. We thought it would mean a lot to a lot of people." In 2003, Tony Kushner and Mark Harris held a Commitment Ceremony attended by George C. Wolfe, who said that when Tony said, "I do," that was the first time Tony ever answered a question with two words. Also in attendance were Mike Nichols, Diane Sawyer, Kathleen Chalfant, and Larry Kramer, among 150 family and friends. When Tony met Mark, he was taken by his perfect grammar. "That was a turn-on," he quipped. Both homebodies who shun the limelight, Mark Harris and Tony Kushner have been together for eighteen years, and are committed to monogamy and to one another. "It's enormously meaningful to me to know that I have a partner for everything that comes along in life. I think life is very tough and the challenges don't get any easier, they get more and more formidable the older you get and the resources in life get less and less. I know emotionally for me, being married, having a husband, having made that commitment to somebody else and having somebody else make that commitment to me makes life less scary, more fun."

Marriage was not official when Mark Harris and Tony Kushner got married in New York City, so, in 2008, they snuck away to Provincetown, where they own a home, and were married by a Provincetown Police Force patrolwoman

and Justice of the Peace at the Town Hall. Tony Kushner
and Mark Harris quietly made their commitment legal.

On the coasts, whatever label you choose to identify yourself
as, the contemporary world is infinitely more welcoming
than it was when Tony Kushner was a young reluctant
cellist in his father's Governor's Program for Gifted Children's
orchestra. Kushner was already part of the post-Stonewall
generation. It took some courage to be an openly gay
playwright in the early '80s and '90s, but certainly not the
same bravery it took to riot at the Stonewall Inn in 1969 or
to march with the Mattachine Society in 1950. Much like
the intimidating tactics in Uganda today, gay men found
at gay bars or marching for gay rights could be arrested,
exposed in the newspapers, fired, divorced, denied visitation
rights, beat up, or murdered. A lot of barriers for LGBTQ
writers, African-American writers, women writers, and
writers with disabilities have since been knocked down.
It doesn't mean that there are no barriers. So Kushner's
advice to young queer writers would be: "Embrace your
difference. Don't try to erase it. Recognize that the pariah
status is something visited upon you, not intrinsic to you.
Don't try to efface yourself in the process of becoming more
acceptable to those who harbor antipathy towards you
because you weaken yourself and become more vulnerable
and in the end, they're not going to treat you well anyway.
You need to be strong and make community with other
people. The thing that worries me about Millennials is the
atomization of political action. Everyone is so individualized
now, oppression is only expressed on a very granular, micro
level. But I'm a true believer in the power of community

and the solidarity with minority communities coming together to force change."

Kushner is even more adamant about the basic role of the artist: "The only thing an artist has to do is try and tell the truth." The forces against telling the truth come from without and from within. Those from within, in Kushner's experience, are more devious and treacherous and harder to recognize. "There's the voice inside that says *you're garbage and nobody should ever really listen to you.* There's the voice that says *you should copy someone successful.* Then, you lie because you think it's a popular point of view. You warp your version of the truth about life because you think you'll get more Twitter followers," he explained.

Kushner doesn't Tweet and doesn't read the critics. His husband filters the reviews and shares the positive ones with him. He has a thin skin and can get really upset if people say nasty things to him in the theater lobby after a show.

"It's enormously meaningful to me to know that I have a partner for everything that comes along in life. I think life is very tough and the challenges don't get any easier, they get more and more formidable the older you get and the resources in life get less and less. I know emotionally for me, being married, having a husband, having made that commitment to somebody else and having somebody else make that commitment to me makes life less scary, more fun."

Tony Kushner

He would be demolished by critics. He finds writing hard and is not good at short pieces, so 140 characters would be daunting. Mark's the journalist and brilliant at Twitter, so he lets Tony know the good stuff. Sounds like a marriage made in heaven? "You'd have to ask him, but I'm incredibly happy," Tony said.

Maarten Mourik

Author, Singer and Songwriter, Photographer

Independent Theater and Documentary Film Director

In a city with more bicycles than citizens, it is no wonder that Maarten Mourik cycled from the Canal District over to our meeting in De Pijp, Amsterdam, the Netherlands. Maarten's photo-essay book, *Urban Nature,* by *Kader Adam,* www.kaderadam.com, a word that derives from the word kader or cadre and Adam, man, or shorthand for Amsterdam, just came out. Mourik led a collective whose goal was to depict ordinary gay life among contemporary gay men, while focusing on daily life, to go under the surface of daily life. "These are not models, just regular gay folks; however it would be a lie to say that these are just regular people because they're better looking than that. They're young, so the binding thing is that they haven't settled yet. That often happens before you're thirty. People, especially men, are focused mostly on themselves before the age of thirty," he said. Mourik shot the majority of photos for the book, available online.

Why did Maarten write the book? He wanted not only to share stories of everyday gay men, but he wanted to begin a dialogue. An honest dialogue with honest stories, not just one about successful role models or romantic love, but stories about regular lives. In one story, a couple of young men like to go to the airport and watch planes depart. In another, a guy is an erotic actor to earn extra money. Another young gay man still lives at home, doesn't get along with his father, and is trying to find a roommate so he can move out. The book reflects the multicultural and transient nature of the gay community—Muslims and Christians, Black and White, Asian and Dutch; one-night stands, loneliness at home and in the closet, hook-ups and serious relationships. The photos were shot in Amsterdam, the UK, and Australia.

It is not surprising that Maarten, named after his father and grandfather, became an artist. His father was a Dutch poet, writer, and UNESCO ambassador. His father exposed the role of Jorge Zorreguieta, then Minister of Agriculture during General Videla's dictatorship and "Dirty War," deemed responsible for 30,000 deaths, disappearances, torture, and babies stolen during Argentina's civil war. Zorreguieta was the father of today's Queen Maxima, Dutch queen married to King Willem. Maarten's mother was an early feminist and journalist.

When Maarten was nine, his parents divorced. He moved back from Bonn, Germany, where his father was stationed at the time, to Amsterdam with his mother and new stepfather. "I was unhappy about the whole thing and feeling powerless. My constitution made me retreat into myself. I am an introvert. As an artist, I have stories to tell but can't put into words over coffee, so I write a song, write a book or write a piece of music. My family setting was not completely safe, so as a child I felt wary and kept my distance. Fortunately, I found a way to express myself through the arts," Maarten explained.

Maarten was a member of Montezuma's Revenge, a successful a capella singing group that toured Europe, mostly the Netherlands and Germany, to wide acclaim. They played several venues in New York City as well, and even got a pleasant review in *Variety*. As a solo singer, Maarten's voice is a Dutch male version of Adele, soulful and deep.

First as an independent theater director, including several major productions in the Netherlands (*The Last 5 Years*,

Montezuma's Revenge, Vroeger of Later, and *Adele Boemendaal*), Mourik devoted his life to the arts. His work has been called "sleek and playful." He considers himself an actor's director. His written work is in the style of the Italian *fotoromanzo,* translated as a "photo love story."

When Maarten met his husband, German oncologist Heinz Josef, twenty-two years ago, he gradually fell in love. The match of the ebullient, warm and expressive Dutch (with one Jewish grandfather) and the reserved, socially-conscious German farm family was a match "truly made here on earth, with grit, sweat and tears," and one that has stood the test of time.

Maarten is not without an interest in science. He studied biophysics and biochemistry at the University of Amsterdam. He was interested in the physics of sound and music. Music is really vibrating air, and he wanted to understand how that was possible. He was interested in the physics of sound and music: if music is just vibrating air, then how is it possible that it touches emotions?

"I took the long way home, the very long way home and I'm still taking the long way home," he said. It's difficult to make a living as an artist, even in Holland. For a long time, Maarten survived on Montezuma's Revenge. He was both sensible and lucky with financial matters and created a buffer to survive lesser times. When he doesn't have enough, he has the good fortune of depending on his very generous husband. Together, they collaborate to have a rich, if not expensive, life. Instead of a 5-star hotel, they might take a bicycle vacation. Instead of going out for expensive meals, he and his husband usually cook at home and host dinner parties with close friends and family.

For a long time, Maarten "stews in his own suds," a Dutch expression for those times when one broods within and solo. "I've basically always known as soon as I came to some kind of consciousness that I was gay, but it took me awhile to share that. Though my mother used to say, 'If you bring home a boyfriend or a girlfriend '" That was the text, but then there was subtext that cautioned me not to disclose that I was gay. Until I fell head-over-heels in love with my first love which brought me out of the closet. I found that it was important and I needed to share that with friends and family."

His father's only response when Maarten told him he was gay was that his father would regret not having grandchildren through Maarten, but having said that, it was really OK. He did, however, have a half-brother who gave his father a grandson named Maarten Malvik Mourik.

Now, with his book on *Urban Nature,* introduced at Amsterdam Pride in August of 2016, he's finding new ways to connect with his audience, particularly online. The book is a slow read, but there is an option on the Website to "share your story" in words, photos, podcasts, or videos. "I think for the reader, they will recognize themselves in my book more than in selfies. Looking at Facebook posts, gay guys think, 'Oh, they're all so happy. Why am I not partying every night? Why am I so boring and nobody loves me? Why am I not laughing as persistently and joyously as all my friends?' If you constantly see other people only happy or lounging in Cambodia, it must make you very unhappy," he explained.

Maarten's latest idea is to work on a documentary about the Orlando PULSE nightclub shootings, called *Orlando Spring*. He's seeking funding for the film project.

As every artist does, he's constantly seeking new ways to express himself. He's always working something out in his art.

For the next generation of gay men, Maarten has this advice: "Probably that sex is a lot less important than you may think."

"As an artist, I have
stories to tell but can't
put into words over
coffee, so I write a song,
write a book or write
a piece of music. My
family setting was
not completely safe, so
as a child I felt wary
and kept my distance.
Fortunately, I found a
way to express myself
through the arts."

Maarten Mourik

Laurie Rubin: And Now I See

Blind Mezzo Soprano and

Co-Founder, Ohana Arts, Honolulu, HI

Frederica von Stade, the great Opera mezzo soprano, has
asked her to join the star on stage to sing duets. Kenny
Loggins enlisted her as his backup singer when she was
twelve. *NY Times* classical music critic Anthony Tommasini
praised her "compelling artistry and communicative power."
LA Times critic Josef Woodard lauded her "charismatic,
multi-textured performance." Her voice has been called
radiant by London critics. For all Laurie Rubin's accolades,
she did not get the roles her voice warranted at the New
York Metropolitan Opera or, even, at the Yale Graduate
School of Music.

Born blind, Laurie Rubin had many obstacles to overcome to
become the acclaimed mezzo soprano singer she is because,
according to her mother, "directors wouldn't cast her because
they were afraid she'd fall off the stage. Laurie's never fallen
off a stage, while many sighted performers have tripped."

She's played Lincoln Center, Carnegie Hall, and Wigmore
Hall in London. As an undergraduate at the esteemed
Oberlin College & Conservatory, she was cast in the lead
role in Rossini's *La Cenerentola, Cinderella or Goodness
Triumphant.* "It was incredible getting to perform an
amazing role. I felt like Cinderella. I felt like people didn't
quite understand me, especially in middle and high school.
I experienced a lot of passive-aggressive bullying. The
other kids were afraid to interact with me, the only blind
student. They just didn't know the first thing about how
I fit onto the social totem pole. When I went to college,
I met all these friends. A director took a chance and
believed I could perform on stage. I think Cinderella is all
about somebody needing to be believed in, that special

mentor, that special love. Many times during rehearsal, I would start crying because it reminded me so much of my own life," Laurie explained.

Undaunted, Laurie Rubin got a Guide Dog and went all over New York City auditioning for opera roles. While she had some successes, it was nearly impossible to overcome the prejudices of most big-time directors. In 2004, Rubin attended a workshop with John Harbison and Dawn Upshaw. The workshop was at Carnegie Hall. Rubin's composer wrote a piece for her called *Target*, a cacophony of new music. Gordon Beeferman was in the audience and cast Rubin as the lead in *Rat Land*, an original New York City Opera where the main character felt so at odds with her family that she saw them as rats in her increasingly devolved psychological state. *NY Times* critic Tommasini called the opera, "complex and daringly modern "Mr. Beeferman's music, with its skittish melodic lines and pungent atonal harmony, is gritty, fidgety and intriguing." The artistic team is still hoping the opera will be staged around the country.

Never one to be told she cannot do something, since her parents—a toy company CEO father and homemaker mother—always taught her she could do anything she put her mind to, Laurie Rubin has been making and selling jewelry to supplement her arts career. With her wife, Jenny Taira, a classical clarinetist and pianist she met while at Oberlin, Rubin and Jenny's sister Cari Lee, founded Ohana Arts. Jenny, a fourth-generation Japanese-American from Hawaii, and Laurie collaborate on songs and musicals seamlessly. Maybe it's astrology—Laurie's a Scorpio and Jenny's a Cancer—but they often have the same artistic sensibilities and even the same themes for musicals. Their latest musical, *Peace on Your Wings,* is the story of famed Japanese Hiroshima survivor Sadako Sasaki, who died of leukemia from radiation poisoning at age twelve. Before she died, she tried to make a thousand cranes for peace. Legend has it that if the maker of a thousand cranes finishes the task, he or she will be granted a wish. Sasaki is honored in Hiroshima with a statue for her brave and high-minded dreams despite her own suffering. Ohana Arts performed the musical in Hawaii to critical acclaim. The cast of *Peace on Your Wings* is made up of youth, ages seven to seventeen. From 2016 to 2020, Rubin and Taira will be taking the musical to the mainland for performances all over the country. In 2020, it will be the 75th anniversary of the atomic bombing of Hiroshima and Nagasaki. Momentum with this play is building up to that year.

Ohana in Hawaiian means family—extended and universal family, not merely biological family. In setting up Ohana Arts, "we wanted to make sure people knew they were part of a performing arts family. Our mission is to cultivate peace through the universal language of the arts. So Ohana already has that sense of family and love and peace," Rubin explained.

Laurie Rubin is also an author. She wrote the book, *Do You Dream in Color? Insights from an Unsighted Girl.* She delved into her lonely years as the only blind student mainstreamed in middle and high school. Even in Hebrew school, those adolescent years were isolating as pre-teens and teens were struggling with their own identities and had little time for a fellow blind student. One "friend" told her she'd never be like the other kids; she'd never have romance because she couldn't see the moonlight. She'd never hold a job or be able to look into her lover's eyes. In response, Laurie Rubin, along with Jenny Taira, wrote what has become her signature song, "The Girl I Am," which she performs for schools and

Musical composer/producer and wife, Jenny Taira (top second from left) and lyricist/producer Laurie Rubin (top left) with Peace on Your Wings Cast of Ohana Arts, Hawaii.

Photo by Marc Orbito

girls choruses around the country, even in remote towns like Rock Springs, Wyoming. Ninety percent of the girls in the audience were crying, many actually sobbing. Laurie Rubin performed for the Rock Springs Girls Choir and the San Francisco Girls Chorus, with Jenny Taira accompanying Rubin on piano. The responses were, "Thank you so much for writing a song like that. Thank you for letting us know it gets better."

It does get better and Laurie Rubin is testament to that. She and Jenny Taira have been together fourteen years and were married in 2013 in her mother's backyard in Los Angeles. Everyone came—her only brother, Brian, who's also gay, her father now living in Utah, her mom, Jenny's family from Hawaii, grandparents, relatives, and friends. Her mom was always fine with Laurie being gay. Her father had a hard time with her older brother, but then had a friend in Utah who had a gay son, so he became okay with it. "He was happy at my wedding and he was happy at my brother's wedding. Eventually he got it," Rubin said.

Neither of Laurie's parents are musical. As her father says, he loves to play the stereo. Her grandparents loved listening to opera. Yet, they recognized Laurie's talent. As a child taking piano lessons, Laurie hated to practice but loved to sing along with her piano teacher's playing. Finally, the piano teacher told Laurie's parents, Laurie can really sing and she loves it, so her parents got Laurie voice lessons which they supported for her from an early age.

Laurie's parents took her and her brother everywhere when they were children—snow skiing, water skiing, white water

rafting, camping. Laurie credits them with her confidence: "I definitely think that having the boost from early childhood was helpful. Without that, it would have been really hard to move through the middle and high school periods. I have friends who never strived for what they truly wanted to do. For me, my parents always taught me to set my sights as high as possible. That really, really helped me." Eventually, as with every artist, it came down to Laurie's own resilience. She had to believe in herself when the world did not show faith in her.

Jenny Taira's Japanese-American family in Hawaii have completely embraced Laurie as Jenny's wife and life partner. So much so that Laurie feels comfortable calling Jenny's mom for advice. Jenny's dad calls Laurie his daughter.

As artists, Jenny and Laurie share a special bond, but it is not without conflict or artistic differences. They quibble like all artists do. Each have their own ideas. But they have learned to compromise. As two artists, financially, it's ridiculous how little money they make. With artists, it's either you make little money or you make tons and tons of money. There's very little middle ground. Fortunately, both are teachers and visiting artists, so they manage to stay afloat financially by using all their talents and skills.

Ohana Arts began in 2010 in Honolulu with twenty kids. In 2016, there are more than eighty kids and the age group expanded from eight to eighteen to six to twenty-four. Instead of one show a year, they do four to five. Now they are performing in LA and New York and, soon, the SF Bay Area, and hope to attract students from the mainland to their summer arts programs in Hawaii.

Just thirty-eight, Rubin has many more musicals to write, songs to sing, and operas to perform. For young queer artists, she would advise, "If you have a hard time expressing who you are or being who you are, know that the best thing you could do for yourself is to find a mentor. Find the people in your life who can help bring out your best self. One of our friend's younger sisters was having a hard time being gay because she lives in a suburb. He told her, 'You've got to meet Jenny and Laurie.' His sister needed to know that there were functional gay relationships because she'd never been around them. So I would say that it's important to get out of your comfort zone and find that place to be yourself. You have to seek out your own family if you don't have it where you live."

"If you have a hard time expressing who you are or being who you are, know that the best thing you could do for yourself is to find a mentor. Find the people in your life who can help bring out your best self."

Laurie Rubin

Colm Toibin: Irish Treasure

Short-Listed for the Man Booker Prize for Fiction, Three Times for:
The Blackwater Lightship, The Master and
The Testament of Mary

Novels: *Nora Webster, Brooklyn, The Story of the Night, The
South, The Heather Blazing,* etc.
Winner, *Hawthorden Prize, Nora Webster*

Nonfiction: *Love in a Dark Time*

It's an American holiday, but Colm Toibin is wearing a white shirt with his sleeves rolled up, ready to work. When he speaks, he holds his head in his hand as though he is holding up the world. His own world came crashing down when he was eight years old and his father, only one of three students from County Wexford to win university scholarship and a teacher in the Christian Brothers' school in Enniscorthy for thirty years, took ill. Colm was shipped off to an aunt's house and never saw his mother once during his months-long exile. When Colm's father died, he was twelve and began to both stammer and write. He was so far down in his classes that there were frequent discussions of his working in a drapery shop—the loftiest ambition those around him could see for him. That all changed at St. Peter's Boarding School, where Colm discovered reading. He devoured books and went on to graduate in English from University College Dublin. It's ironic that words saved him when he grew up after his father's death, in a world of silence in his widowed mother's home.

Barack Obama and his daughters, Sasha and Malia, bought his latest book in a Washington, DC bookshop. Hollywood adapted one of his novels. Britain honored his work with one of its oldest literature awards. Still, he writes in obscurity on a new novel set in ancient Greece and can go totally unrecognized at the East Los Angeles neighborhood Trader Joe's. He spends his days writing, sitting in the garden, and doing pretty much nothing else. Not a television watcher, he prefers observing real life around him. He's only been to Hollywood three times while the film adapted from his novel, *Brooklyn*, was being shown and given Academy Award nominations for Best Film, Best Actress, and Best Adapted

Screenplay. His novel, *Nora Webster,* was awarded the 2015 British Hawthornden Prize; his was the only Irish novel nominated. "Totally nice dinner in London. Everyone there was English and everyone there had read the book. It's such a gentle book, not a book filled with obvious excitement. A very Irish book. Getting that award mattered enormously to me," Toibin said.

Nora Webster drew a portrait of a grieving mother in rural Ireland in the late 1960s. It was with all the details, "absolute and true," that Toibin inhabited the character. After not sleeping well and suffering problems at work, the character walks the beach she used to walk with her deceased husband and says to a nun passing, in one of her only spiritual and searching moments, "We walk among them sometimes, the ones who have left us. They are filled with something none of us knows. It is a mystery."

Toibin writes a lot about exile and home. His story of Henry James in nineteenth-century England, *The Master,* won the International Impac Dublin Literary Award, the world's most valuable literary prize ($150,000) for a single work of fiction, chosen from nominations by public librarians worldwide. He was the first Irish writer to win. *The Master* was also short-listed for the 2004 Man Booker Prize. The fictional Henry James says, "For the first time in years, he felt the deep sadness of exile, knowing that he was alone here, an outsider "" Toibin, too, has felt the sting of the outsider. When he first went to Spain in 1975 and during elections in 1976 when he couldn't vote, he felt left out of conversations. Of the plight of the immigrant, he says, "I think anyone who goes through that on any given day and anyone who doesn't go through that forms a perspective. For James in England, no matter what he did, he was always considered an American. Even though he'd lived there for so many years and became loyal to the place. Still, it wasn't his country."

In *The Blackwater Lightship,* short-listed for the Man Booker Prize in 1999, Toibin tackles the subject of AIDS in the character of Declan, returning home to be cared for by his family at the end of his life. Asked if there was a backlash against the book, Toibin was emphatic, "Oh, God, no. Oh no." No matter the shock of realizing their son was gay and dying, no Irish family would ever turn out their son. Though Toibin witnessed the devastation of AIDS, he never witnessed a family turning its back on a son with AIDS in Ireland. He hadn't seen it in America either, but he had heard that it happened.

Colm Toibin never discussed being gay in detail with his mother when she was alive. Once his mother asked his sister not if he was gay, but, "Is Colm happy?" Colm said, "That was nice." He's not given to the American practice of returning home full of recriminations for a sixty-or seventy-year-old parent when one is thirty or forty and uncovers the effects of loss and absence from one's childhood. Best to "move on," and Colm has, taking refuge in the blank page, the hard chair, the empty wall. From that well, Toibin has drawn some of the most arresting portrayals of women — three generations of women coping with the newfound knowledge that their grandson/son/brother is both gay and dying of AIDS in *The Blackwater Lightship;* the young, bewildered immigrant in *Brooklyn;* the crazy sister in *The Master;* the descent into grief's darkest basement and the awakening of the newly solo widow in *Nora Webster;* and the portrait of a woman who has watched her son vilified, tortured, and hung from a cross in *The Testament of Mary,* a novel and a play.

Brooklyn, Academy Award-nominated film,
Adapted from Colm Toibin's
novel of the same name, starring Saoirse Ronan

One night, Meryl Streep asked to have dinner with Colm
Toibin in New York after she had completed the audiobook,
The Testament of Mary, short-listed for the 2013 Man Booker
Prize. One line stands out when read by the most-decorated
American actress: "If you want witnesses, then I am one
and I can tell you now, when you say that he redeemed the
world, I will say that it was not worth it. It was not worth
it." Toibin was very happy that Streep wanted to record his
book, and said she did quite a good job and found her very
nice in person. But he did not sound starstruck in any way.

Saoirse Ronan played the lead role in *Brooklyn* when
she was just twenty years old. Though she'd appeared in
other films—*The Lovely Bones* and *The Grand Budapest
Hotel*—she'd never played an Irish character before. And
she performed it just perfectly. The role called for someone
who "pulls in the light. There's an awful lot of light involved
in that book. And she had to have a presence. When the
camera was on her, she knew exactly what she was to do,"
Colm explained. For the film, Ronan garnered an Academy
Award nomination for Best Actress.

Colm Toibin is both ambassador and agitator for his home
country. During the marriage equality referendum in Ireland,
Toibin wrote, spoke, and agitated for its passage. Ireland was
the first country in the world to vote for marriage equality
in May of 2015. The prior law permitted Civil Partnership.
In the lead-up to the referendum, there was a big split in
the gay marriage movement—one group, the Moderates,
wanted to settle for Civil Partnership and work towards
more rights, and the other group, the Radicals, wanted
nothing less than Marriage Equality. In 2014, the leaders

of the Moderates (Brian) and the Radicals (Grainne) got together and agreed to stop the argument. Together, they sought the best outside advice in running a referendum in Ireland. The consultants worked free of charge and advised that the supporters should take a softer tone and focus on the personal, not the abstract. No one interviewed on TV was to get angry, no matter what the opposition said or did. Toibin had to tamp down his natural assuredness in the radio spots he did for the movement. Door-to-door canvassing, quite common in Ireland, was to be done with a family member if possible. The LGBTQ person was to say nothing and the mother or father was to ask the voter for a vote for his or her son's or daughter's equality. Ads featured families of gay people and pleas for equality. Just before the vote, the well-respected former President of Ireland for fourteen years, a lifelong Catholic, Mary McAleese, asked for the vote for her twin children, one of whom was gay. The referendum was successful. In front of Dublin Castle, once the seat of British rule, supporters flooded the square for the overwhelming 62 percent vote in favor. For Colm, that was the most moving moment. That, and attending the wedding of two of his friends who had gotten together in their twenties, and been together forty years.

Still, bullying remains a big problem in Ireland. A 2009 Irish study, Supporting LGBT Lives, found that 50 percent of young gay people under the age of twenty-five have seriously thought of ending their lives, and 20 percent have attempted suicide. Justin McAleese, the Irish President's son, despite growing up in an affirming household, did not feel he could come out. He kept his sexuality secret until he was twenty-one. In a country where 90 percent of all public

As far as advice Colm Toibin would give to a young LGBTQ person in Ireland, he said, "I would ask for their advice. When you consider how the 2015 Marriage Equality referendum was conducted, it was conducted with great civility. There was a way in which the whole country of Ireland was engaged in the debate. And the images of gay people were very positive."

Colm Toibin

schools are run by the Catholic Church, it is hard to find a welcoming environment where being gay is okay, normal, or even cool. In single gender schools, bullying is epidemic, especially "if the ethos of that school is fundamentally Catholic. Bullying stops when being gay is seen as normal, absolutely fine. Then, bullying stops. Some gays have found safe havens in coed schools because the girls take care of them and condemn homophobia of any sort," Toibin asserted.

As far as advice Colm Toibin would give to a young LGBTQ person in Ireland, he said, "I would ask for their advice. When you consider how the 2015 Marriage Equality referendum was conducted, it was conducted with great civility. There was a way in which the whole country of Ireland was engaged in the debate. And the images of gay people were very positive."

Icons

1. **Sidney Grant**, Founder of Harlem's Ballroom Basix and USA Tango Champion, Dance Teacher for film, *Mona Lisa Smile,* starring Julia Roberts, Maggie Gyllenhaal, Marcia Gay Harden, and Kirsten Dunst; coached Antonio Banderas for *Take the Lead,* and appeared in documentary film, *Mad Hot Ballroom*

2. **Kate Kendell,** Executive Director of National Center for Lesbian Rights since 1996

3. **Bishop Karen Oliveto, PhD,** first openly LGBT Bishop in the United Methodist Church, 2016 - Present

4. **Leanne Pittsford,** Founder of Lesbians Who Tech

5. **Robbie Tristan Szelei,** Hungarian Activist on neo-Nazi "hit list;" Organizer of Pride Parade and Mr. Gay Europe in Budapest; World Champion Ballroom, Latin and Show Dancer

6. **Ardel Haefele-Thomas, PhD,** Chair of LGBT Studies at City College of San Francisco, First Accredited LGBT Studies Program in California and One of the First in the US; Author of First Undergraduate Transgender Textbook in the World, *Introduction to Transgender Studies* (Harrington Press, Columbia University Press, 2017)

7. **Louisa Wall,** New Zealand Maori Member of Parliament and Author of the Successful Marriage Amendment; New Zealand Rugby Player of the Year; Gold-Winning World Champion Rugby Team Member

8. **John "Long Jones" Abdallah Wambere,** Ugandan Activist in US on Asylum; GLAAD Media Award-Winner as part of Cast for Documentary, *Call Me Kuchu*

9. **Rick Welts,** Highest-Ranking Openly Gay Sports Executive; President of Golden State Warriors, National Basketball Association 2015 Champions

10. **Claudia Brind-Woody,** Fifth Highest-Ranking LGBTQ Executive in the World; VP of Global Intellectual Property Licensing at IBM, based in UK; Former Assistant to Coach Pat Summitt, University of Tennessee

Sidney Grant: From Hollywood to Harlem

Founder of Ballroom Basix

National USA Tango Champion

First Gay Couple, Sidney Grant and his now husband,
Claudio Marcelo Vidal, to make it into
the Finals of the 2016 USA Tango Competition
Dance Teacher, *Mona Lisa Smile*
Coached award-winning ballroom dance
students for film, *Take the Lead*
Featured in documentary film, *Mad Hot Ballroom*

When Sidney Grant was climbing the three-story walk-up in a seedy neighborhood in New York City, he wondered if he'd made the right decision to cancel his private dance lesson for the promise of an opportunity to work on a film. When he knocked on the steel frame door and Julia Roberts answered, "Welcome, you must be Sidney. Hi, I'm Julia Roberts," he knew he'd made the right decision. He was soon hired to teach the leading ladies—Julia Roberts, Marcia Gay Harden, Maggie Gyllenhaal, and Kirsten Dunst—to ballroom dance for the dance scenes in the 1950s coming-of-age film depicting life at Wellesley College, *Mona Lisa Smile*. He even appeared in the film, earning his Screen Actors Guild card, for this feminist film of 2003.

Why would a budding Hollywood actor and son of a theater director, who once appeared on *Good Morning America* with Antonio Banderas for his role in coaching the award-winning ballroom dance champions from the Bronx featured in the film *Take the Lead*, eschew life on the stage and in film for the grit of Harlem classrooms? Why would a ballroom and Tango dance champion work in public schools in the inner city? Why would Grant want to teach children who listen to hip hop and rap to waltz across a gym floor? In a word, bullying. That's what Sidney and his twin brother experienced when their mother made them take tap as seven-year-olds and all the other kids made fun of them. To this day, when a kid calls him a "faggot," Sidney has to summon all the self-control within him to make this a teaching moment. He de-personalizes the comment by asking the young man, "Is that how we speak to one another as ladies and gentlemen?" All the children are addressed as Mr. or Ms. The kid will mumble something and I'll say, 'I'm sorry I didn't hear you'. I hold the mirror of accountability to the child to show that gentlemen do not treat me, or their teachers, or one another that way. I instill classroom management skills in all my teaching artists. We encourage our students to behave in a way that is civil and respectful," Grant said.

Dr. Dance—Sidney Grant—and students,
Ballroom Basix Ball.

Photo by Jason Russo

The founder of Ballroom Basix, an arts education program
for NYC public school sixth graders, teaches "Manners
matter with every step." So the first thing the Leaders learn
to say is, "May I have this dance with you, please?" And
the Followers respond, "Of course you may, thank you so
much." The Leaders then take the Follows on the arm and
escort them into the dance circle. How did Sidney Grant get
the boys to act in such a gentlemanly way? First, instead of
forcing the boys to touch the girls, he asks all the partnered
dancers to give him a High Ten. Once Leads and Follows
are touching hands, palm to palm, Sidney instructs, "Now,
HOLD!" And the way Sidney persuades the boys to escort
the Follows onto the dance floor is that he tells them to flex
their biceps and, now, turn that upside down, creating a
space for the Follow to link arms. "Eye-to-eye, hand-to-hand,
when did we lose that? When did that go out of style?"
Sidney says of his partner dancing workshops in schools in
Harlem, Brooklyn, Queens, and the Bronx.

Grant began his program in 2008 after seven years as an
instructor with Dancing Classrooms and artistic director
and co-founder of the American Ballroom Theater Youth
Company. The program was featured in the documentary
Mad Hot Ballroom. Of the film, Grant says, "A movie
is one thing, three different schools from three different
demographics and following those schools throughout the
quarterfinals, the semifinals and the finals, makes for a great
plot line for a movie. It makes for a miserable experience for
the children." Many children who lost were crushed. They
collapsed on the floor sobbing inconsolably. Sidney's a firm
believer that the arts "allow our spirits to shine and this
is especially useful for children as a tool for self-expression

and as a tool for creative development. It's night and day from competition. If you're just giving a child the venue to shine, they don't have to win, they just have to shine. So our mantra in some of the toughest schools is, 'We don't beat the other school, we meet the other school.'" The Ballroom Basix Bash is an annual fundraiser that involves two sixth grade populations from different schools. They come together. The Leads ask Follows they don't know for a dance. After that, the dancing is rotational, so the kids will dance with some students they've never met and some of their own classmates. Sidney asks, "What could be more important in life than learning to be comfortable meeting a stranger? The finale gives kids a real-life tool, not a place where they have to out-dress, out-dish or out-perform their peers."

In 2016, Ballroom Basix will have served more than 10,000 kids from neighborhoods where gangs recruit sixth graders, children live with violence, and adolescents get pregnant in epic proportions. Teachers work with kids, through the vehicle of ballroom and Latin ballroom dancing—Merengue, Foxtrot, Tango, Rumba, Swing, Waltz, Salsa, and Cha-Cha-Chá—to teach "Conduct, Camaraderie and Character" or "Fun, Fitness and Fancy Footwork." Is it working? To hear a former Harlem PS 149 principal tell it, "Some of our middle school kids are pretty tough, so it amazed me how Mr. Sid's inclusive, non-competitive approach to partner dancing reached each student so powerfully." Another sixth grade teacher in Harlem had this to say: "One of my students who was very shy...all of a sudden started movin' and shakin' and it was like a different student came out! There was light in her eyes, and a smile, and the students even looked at her differently than they do in the classroom environment."

Dr. Dance, so named by the famed sexologist Dr. Ruth Westheimer, tells another story with tears in his eyes. One of the Harlem mothers took Dr. Dance aside and told him that her son had completely transformed into a gentleman since taking Ballroom Basix in school. She tells the story of how she had to move from the suburbs back to Harlem when her husband was imprisoned and her sixth grade son began running with gangs. However, ever since taking Ballroom Basix, he came home delighted with Dr. Dance and his Ballroom Basix. He held doors open for his mother, addressed her respectfully and escorted her on the streets of Spanish Harlem with the poise he'd learned to escort Follows onto the dance floor and stepped away from the wrong crowd.

The reward for the kids doing the hard work of Ballroom Basix every workshop is The Barn Dance, a rotational dance Sid learned at the gay *Big Apple Ranch* club in New York. Only, instead of dancing to Country Western music as Sidney first did, the kids dance to Lady Gaga or Katy Perry.

When asked if Sidney had any data to show that Ballroom Basix reduces bullying, his eyes lit up. In Fall of 2016, Ballroom Basix, in collaboration with a local college, will be designing a study for the South Bronx that he anticipates will validate all the anecdotal evidence from parents, teachers, and principals that this program reduces bullying. Bullying is epidemic. It's tough to go in and effect cultural change among middle school students. That first year of middle school when kids come in from many different elementary schools and try to fit in is crucial to a child's self-esteem and relationship to lifelong learning. If this message of "poise and politeness is being instilled artistically in thousands of public school children, I can't think of a better way to spend my time," Grant said.

What teachers like best about Ballroom Basix is the learning aspect in every workshop. Students learn about language, culture, geography, spelling, music, math, and manners.

Claudio Marcelo Vidal and Sidney Grant, first gay USA Tango Finalists.

Photo by Don An

When the students learn Merengue, they first learn how to spell it and that it originates from the Dominican Republic. The Dominican kids beam with pride when they talk about their internationally-acclaimed dance in Spanish. The Foxtrot, African-American kids learn, began with them in the 1930s. Tango is from Argentina and Uruguay. Rumba is from Cuba, and Swing is from the African-American Harlem Renaissance. Salsa hails from Puerto Rico, Columbia, and NYC, and Cha-Cha-Chá from Cuba. Teachers discuss the history of the dances in every single class. They spell it out. They ask questions in Spanish and English.

How did a nice Jewish boy from upstate New York learn Spanish so well? Sidney's paternal grandparents moved from Chicago to San Miguel de Allende, and the family took an educational road trip from New Jersey to Mexico. There, at age eleven, both boys started adult Spanish classes at Instituto de Allende, and returned again at age fourteen. Throughout middle school and high school, Sidney Grant studied Spanish. He minored in Spanish at Rutgers University. As fate would have it, Grant met his future husband, Claudio Marcelo Vidal, at a tango competition in Buenos Aires. Today, they live in Spanish Harlem and, in 2016, became the first gay couple to compete in and make it into the Finals of the USA Tango Competition. Claudio danced in a white tuxedo and heels, and Sidney in a black tuxedo and spats.

So why did Sidney Grant make the journey from Hollywood to Harlem? "Strongly, at my core, I'm staunchly non-competitive when it comes to the arts. The arts are such an affirmation of one's creativity, self-expression, artistry. It's not

something that requires a medal
or a trophy or a ribbon to validate
"What makes partner dancing so
magical is that there's a synergy,
a harmony between two people
moving to music as seamlessly as
possible with one another."

Marcia Gay Harden is the
honorary chair of the Ballroom
Basix Board. The Brooklyn-born
Chancellor in NYC, Carmen
Fariña, is very pro-arts. Several
City Council members, the
Speaker and the Manhattan
Borough president, have supported
Ballroom Basix with discretionary
funds. And partner dancers
everywhere can support the
program through online donations.

What advice would Sidney Grant
give queer youth in the inner
city? "Find your peers. Be yourself.
And celebrate, don't shrink, from
pursuing the magic of the arts to
transform squalor into splendor."

"To this day, when a
kid calls him a faggot,
Sidney has to summon
all the self-control
within him to make
this a teaching moment.
He de-personalizes the
comment by asking the
young man, "Is that
how we speak to one
another as ladies and
gentlemen?"

Sidney Grant

Kate Kendell, Esq.

Executive Director, National Center for Lesbian Rights
Co-Counsel, Tennessee Case brought before Supreme Court
SCOTUS Decision Legalizing Same-Sex Marriage, June 26, 2015

Kate Kendell grew up Mormon in Ogden, Utah, where the church considers being lesbian a grievous sin. Its immoral behavior is to be abjured. Before coming out to herself, Kendell was active and held many leadership positions— to the extent that girls were allowed to hold leadership positions—in the Mormon Church. She loved the social aspect of the church. All her friends went to church because that's what happens in Mormon communities, where 90 percent of your neighbors and classmates are Mormon. She never had what the church called "testimony." She never quite "bought the story that being a faithful woman was the only way to salvation." She came to consciousness as a feminist first, and then as a lesbian in her late teens. So when she left the church, she didn't have the same traumatic identity or faith crisis her LGBT friends did. When she finally told her mother she was gay, her mother reacted, "The most important thing to me is that you're happy." Kendell's mother saying that made everything possible. It gave Kendell permission to embrace who she was as a lesbian. She had a very close relationship with her mother, so her mother's opinion mattered most. Kendell's father died when she was three, and her mother had married Kate's stepfather who was both racist and given to rages, so she didn't care much what he thought. Her mother's status as a Mormon widow with two small children and no college education, no doubt, influenced her choice of husband. Kate's mother died following a series of strokes, but despite cognitive difficulties, often told friends and neighbors, "Kate's making the world a better place for LGBT people everywhere." Not only did Kate's Mormon mother embrace her lesbian daughter, but she was her greatest champion. She loved Kate unconditionally. This gave her the courage to pursue law school.

Kate Kendell met her current wife, Sandy Holmes, an African-American graduate of Yale University and long-time development associate for ACLU, at an ACLU Conference twenty-three years ago. At the time, Kendell was an ACLU lawyer for Utah, and Holmes was a fundraiser for the San Francisco ACLU office and on the Board of Directors of NCLR. Once a spark was lit at an LGBT Caucus (read: cocktail party), Holmes encouraged Kendell to apply to be Legal Director of NCLR. Kendell got the job and moved to San Francisco.

But partnering with an African-American woman, even in progressive San Francisco, was not without its challenges. "When I told my mother about Sandy, her reaction was, 'Honey, I just think things are going to be harder for you.'" She already felt the lesbian thing was hard enough. But one thing about Sandy, as Kate's family will attest, is that once they met her, they were less interested in Kate, because "Sandy is just such a wonderful, kind, dear and generous person, she just won them over."

Utah has a very, very dominant white culture. "And to be who I wanted to be with Sandy, I was forced to really unpack white privilege, to understand how deep white supremacy goes, how you're either part of dismantling it or complicit in upholding it. To really understand race and racism I feel is one of the most important lessons of my life," said Kate.

In her twenty years as Executive Director of the National Center for Lesbian Rights, recent headlines would be among the highlights of Kendell's legal career. The 2015 SCOTUS landmark decision *Obergefell v. Hodges* ruled that same-sex couples enjoyed the same freedom to marry as all couples. NCLR was co-counsel in the case from Tennessee, one of four cases that led to the *Obergefell* decision.

There have been extreme highs and lows in Kate Kendell's efforts to secure justice for LGBTQ individuals. "The audacity to fight for justice. The perseverance to win" is not just a tagline; NCLR and Kate Kendell, in particular, needed that perseverance. "We won marriage in California in May, 2008. NCLR was lead counsel in that case. Winning marriage in California was the pinnacle of my legal career. It felt like a moment that could change everything for LGBTQ people. Then, when Proposition 8 passed eliminating the right to marry in California in November of 2008, that was the nadir of my career and maybe the most devastating moment of my professional life. It was truly devastating."

On June 26, 2013, the Supreme Court of the United States issued its decision on the appeal of the federal challenge to Prop 8 in *Hollingsworth v. Perry*, ruling that proponents of initiatives such as Proposition 8 did not possess legal standing in their own right to defend the resulting law in federal court, either to the Supreme Court or (previously) to the Ninth Circuit Court of Appeals. Prop 8 was finally overturned.

These legal battles were just a few of the many fought by Kate Kendell and NCLR on the road to the freedom to marry and the assurance of parental rights. These issues are particularly personal to Kate. When Kate and her former partner, Lori, met, Lori's daughter, Emily, was one-years-old.

Kate and Lori were together for twelve years, functioning as co-parents. Kate developed a deep relationship with Emily, yet Kate had no legal parental rights in Utah. When Kate and Lori split up, fortunately, Lori was such a good person that Emily continued to be a part of Kate's life. Now thirty-five, Emily married Heather in 2013 just after a Utah judge

Kate Kendell and Sandy Holmes, together 23 years, and family.

Photo by Dave Allen

ruled in favor of the freedom to marry in a case where
NCLR was co-counsel.

Today, Kate and her wife Sandy have two kids. Kate went
through the second parent adoption process, including a
home study by a social worker, and became son Julian's
legal parent. With their younger daughter, five years later,
the process was more streamlined. On the birth certificates,
the kids are Julian Lucas Kendell Holmes and Arianna
Ashton Kendell Holmes. Julian was born in 1996 and
Arianna in 2001. While it's been one of the most enriching
experiences of Kate's life, being queer parents raising kids of
color, "You really have to learn to be open-hearted about
some of the questions that come up. Julian said once, 'I wish
I had a dad.' And later he told us that he had wished he
had an African-American man as more of a presence in his
life. And I have to step back and ask, *Tell me why you feel
that way.* And not feel blamed or shamed, because that
was not his intent. He was simply expressing a desire for
what was missing. By being open and honest and available,
we now have a grown son and an almost-grown daughter
and when we are together, like on our recent vacation to
Hawaii, our kids both expressed gratitude and appreciation
for our family. No one can give their kids everything, but
one strives to give them what they need." Kate just returned
from dropping off Julian at the University of Maryland for
his sophomore year. There, he finds more of an African-
American community, which is one of the reasons he chose
Maryland. He's taking care of himself. And Arianna is in
an independent school in San Francisco where diversity is
valued and encouraged. Kate's family just attended a Black

Student Union picnic in Berkeley for forty to fifty families attending the same independent SF high school.

Kate's wife, Sandy, sustains her in both her professional and private life. They began their long-distance relationship in a time before cell phones, Skype, and emails, which meant they courted by writing letters and calling long-distance. Seeing each other once a month made every minute count when the two were together. And it gave them time to reflect. "We are the classic Yin and Yang. It's a good match. Her friends realized how much I love her, so they embraced me. She's very grounding. I can be a high-flying Aries and she's a thoughtful Capricorn. I help her get out of her head and become more playful and impetuous and she helps me be more clear-eyed and focused. We laugh a lot. It's truly the best thing that's ever happened to me," Kate said.

This sustaining partnership allows Kendell to take on controversial issues. Recently, NCLR honored Black Lives Matter. They've collaborated with NAACP and other groups committed to racial equity. The fight for true justice goes on. NCLR is working to end conversion therapy. At one time, documented in the film *Latter Days*, Utah Mormon parents sent their children to institutions for electroshock conversion therapy in an attempt to make their gay kids straight. To this day, Mormonism actively seeks to "pray the gay away" with counseling that aims to train gay people to be able to exist in heterosexual marriages, since marriage is a very important tenet of the religion. Kendell and NCLR are fighting to end conversion therapy through legislation, public education, and, if possible, litigation. Employment rights, especially for transgender individuals

"But I truly believe, and it's not just a slogan, that for any queer person, no matter where they live and no matter how hard things are in a particular moment, whether it's family or school mates or community, it will get better. You will find your community. You will be able to be whatever you want to be, so do not let the haters pull you down, because you're going to leave them far behind when you're soaring in whatever endeavor you want."

Kate Kendell

who suffer unemployment rates as high as 40 percent, are on the NCLR docket, along with asylum and immigration rulings, anti-bullying policies and practices, healthcare, housing, marriage benefits, retirement access, senior rights, and sports equity. There are no plans to go international. It is Kendell's feeling and the feeling of the Board that NCLR is expert on US laws and that there are other international organizations more suited to take on those issues. Implied is the sense that though some US laws have changed, public education, social policy, and defense of equal access remain serious concerns throughout the US, particularly in rural areas of the country where the practice of equality is less than perfect.

Today, Kendell is less lawyer and more strategic thinker, advocate, staff cheerleader, fundraiser, and spokesperson. The organization has grown to encompass key experts in all arenas.

Kendell's advice to a young LGBTQ person growing up in

the US today is, "Probably, the sky's the limit. I think this moment is probably the most rich with opportunity for LGBTQ people than any other time in history. That's not to say that there isn't still tremendous homophobia, bigotry and violence and people should always do what they need to do to protect themselves. But I truly believe, and it's not just a slogan, that for any queer person, no matter where they live and no matter how hard things are in a particular moment, whether it's family or school mates or community, it will get better. You will find your community. You will be able to be whatever you want to be, so do not let the haters pull you down, because you're going to leave them far behind when you're soaring in whatever endeavor you want."

Bishop Dr. Karen Oliveto: Christ's Perfect Love

First Openly Lesbian Bishop of the United Methodist Church
Appointed July 15, 2016, Western Jurisdictional Conference

Born on Good Friday in a town called Babylon, is it any wonder Karen Oliveto received the call to ministry for the United Methodist Church (UMC) when she was eleven years old? "I always found church, ever since I was about three or four years old, a place that really felt like home to me. I loved the stories of faith. I loved the Bible. I loved learning about Jesus. I loved the hymns and the music and I loved, most of all, the community that wrapped my sisters and me in love," Karen explained.

A lifelong Methodist, being a "United Methodist is in my DNA. I am a Wesleyan at the core. I understand that the Methodist tradition calls us to great personal and social holiness." That drive to holiness took the Long Island granddaughter of Italian immigrants to Seminary at the Pacific School of Religion in Berkeley, CA, where she received her Master of Divinity in 1983. Oliveto takes the words attributed to UMC founder, John Wesley, to heart: "Do all the good you can. By all the means you can. In all the ways you can. In all the places you can. To all the people you can. As long as ever you can."

Karen Oliveto served as pastor in Bloomville, NY from 1983-1986 and as Campus Minister at San Francisco State University from 1989-1992. Her full immersion into church life came when she served as pastor of the diverse and reconciling congregation of Bethany United Methodist Church in Noe Valley, San Francisco, from 1992-2004. "What I loved about Bethany is that we called each other to greater faithfulness," Karen said. In 2004, she performed nine legal weddings for members of the LGBTQ community during San Francisco's "Winter of Love." Reverend Oliveto performed the first legal wedding for same-gender couples to be held in a United Methodist Church.

For that, she had to answer, as the UMC *Book of Discipline* states in paragraph 304.3: "The practice of homosexuality is incompatible with Christian teaching. Therefore self-avowed practicing homosexuals are not to be certified as candidates, ordained as ministers, or appointed to serve in The United Methodist Church." Further, in paragraph 341.6: "Ceremonies that celebrate homosexual unions shall not be conducted by our ministers and shall not be conducted in our churches." So, Rev. Karen Oliveto was brought to the attention of the local Bishop who required Oliveto to figure out a way for just resolution. The great thing was it didn't go to trial and the complaint was withdrawn. Many jurisdictions, including the Western Jurisdiction, feel this stance against homosexuality, homosexual unions, and homosexual ministers is outdated and out of step with the UMC's tagline of "Open Hearts. Open Minds. Open Doors."

So, Dr. Karen Oliveto, having gotten her PhD in Religion from Drew University, her undergraduate alma mater in 2002, moved on from the middle class, educated, mostly white parish membership of Noe Valley's Bethany to become Academic Dean, from 2004-2008, at the Pacific School of Religion, where she was invited to teach all the required courses for UMC ordination. In 2008, Dr. Oliveto left the comfort of academia to join one of the most vibrant, controversial, and celebrated Methodist churches in America, Glide Memorial Methodist Church. Oliveto's congregation is located in the worst ghetto of San Francisco, the Tenderloin, long known for its prostitutes, drug addicts, and homeless denizens. Unorthodox, co-founders Rev. Cecil Williams and his wife, poet Janice Mirikitani, took the church to the streets. There, they minister to the poor and disenfranchised. Their programs are kept afloat with high-profile fundraisers, an annual ball that attracts Hollywood luminaries and well-known politicians, celebrity volunteers, and Warren Buffet, whose "lunch with" has been auctioned off every year for the past ten years for millions of dollars. "I had to earn my power and authority in ways that don't often happen when you're senior pastor, but I learned a great deal from Janice and Cecil about social justice and ministry. I'm very grateful for the lessons I learned and for my eight years at Glide," Dr. Oliveto said.

Always a powerful orator, Dr. Karen Oliveto spends fifteen to twenty hours a week preparing her sermons. Here's her litmus test: "If I'm bored, I'm going to bore others." So, Oliveto tries to see the human condition and hear what people are saying that resonates with her. She finds that sweet spot between what's going on in the world and people's lives and where God belongs in the intersection between the sacred and the profane.

Oliveto has served on the board of the Reconciling Ministries Network, whose mission is to mobilize United Methodists of all sexual orientations and gender identities to transform the Church and world into the full expression of Christ's inclusive love. "I loved being on the board. This critical movement in the life of UMC gives new life to UMC at a time when more churches are closing than are being built in the US," Oliveto explained.

Her grounding in theology, in the sociology of religion, in the day-to-day practice of urban pastoral care, and in her teaching as adjunct professor of United Methodist Studies at the Pacific School of Religion from 2005-2016, all qualified her as a candidate for Bishop, nominated by the California-Nevada Conference. She was elected Bishop on July 15, 2016, at the Western Jurisdictional conference. Her life office

Robin Ridenour, RN, and Bishop Karen Oliveto on their wedding day, together 17 Years

of Bishop, serving an area in four-year increments with a mandatory retirement age, began September 1, 2016, just outside Denver, Colorado, with the Mountain Sky Area.

Dr. Karen Oliveto is the first openly lesbian Bishop in the United Methodist Church. That makes her both a pioneer and a target. The global Methodist church comprises over 11 million members, with nearly half outside the United States. Even within the US, many have already vilified the Western Jurisdiction for violating church law and appointing an active, married, openly lesbian Bishop. Standing outside Glide Memorial Church in the Tenderloin of San Francisco, homeless and addicted street people lining up for the free meal of the day, Bishop Oliveto had this to say of her appointment: "Together we crossed the threshold into history. We are learning to live in the tension of our differences." After much prayer, discernment, and hard discussion, the Jurisdiction braved the opposition and chose Dr. Karen Oliveto to lead the church forward, to be able to live up to the UMC's stated platform as a welcoming, inclusive church. Dr. Oliveto reflected on one addicted man's plea during a speakout session, where ordinary parishioners can tell their stories at Glide: "Can I trust you with my dignity?" This question informs all Oliveto's encounters going forward. Inclusiveness means all people: gay and straight, old and young, homeless and well-heeled, immigrant and native-born citizen, addicted and healthy, able-bodied and differently-abled, Black and white, Latino and Asian, Native American and Other. That's one lesson she lived at Glide Memorial Methodist Church on Ellis Street in San Francisco.

Dr. Karen Oliveto's decision to heed the call to become a Bishop did not come easily. She resisted offers for several years fearing she would harm the body of Christ, the church, with her acceptance of the post as an open lesbian in a committed relationship of seventeen years. A conference call was set for a Sunday where she had to give a YES or NO answer. She wrestled with her decision, talked extensively with her wife, Robin Ridenour, RN, who finally said to her, "Perfect love casts out all fear." Once she said that, something clicked and Karen said YES to allowing her name to come forward as a candidate for the episcopacy. The Western Jurisdiction of the United Methodist Church affirmed her call by electing her to join the Council of Bishops, where she is certain to face opposition.

How will she deal with that opposition? "I have to do what the Spirit says to do. I will use the tool of love. I think that when I stay rooted in love I can't hurt people. That tool can change us both. So that's the main tool." Could she be brought up on charges and denied her life's work? That's a real possibility, but Oliveto feels the time has come in the church to heed Christ's call to love all.

So Karen and Robin, in the ultimate test of faith, sold their home in the San Francisco Bay Area. Along with her wife, Robin, a UMC deaconess in the California-Nevada conference and nurse anesthetist, Karen Oliveto made the trek across country to just outside Denver, Colorado, where they were welcomed with open arms, arms open as wide as the Rocky Mountain sky. Robin will now be closer to relatives in Colorado and Montana, so she's excited about the move.

Once again, Dr. Oliveto is breaking the stained glass ceiling. Throughout her career, she's come to realize how women are marginalized in professional circles. Women have to work harder. Their voices aren't heard as much. Women face many more challenges in order to become respected leaders. Sexism, as well as homophobia, pervades the church culture. As an Aries, that new ground is nothing new for this braveheart.

She'll continue mentoring and teaching the next generation of ministers and seminarians in her new role. While she'll miss the SF Bay Area, her support network has always been all over the country, and that will continue.

Her advice to young queer Methodists or any queer youth of faith is: "Never forget that you are loved just as you are by a God who will never let you go." So leaning on her gifts and graces, rather than just her sexual orientation, Dr. Karen Oliveto urges LGBTQ ministers and

"Never forget that you are loved just as you are by a God who will never let you go."

Bishop Dr. Karen Oliveto

seminarians to remember, "In all things, God works for good and if you are called, God will make the way. You will find full inclusion and grace. There are many annual conferences in the UMC where you will be embraced for your gifts and graces, not excluded because of your sexual orientation. Go to those places where you will be supported."

Leanne Pittsford: Lesbian Tech Advocate

Founder and CEO
Lesbians Who Tech

She was an unlikely person to start an international phenomenon that draws together 20,000 lesbians in technology in thirty-seven cities around the world. What began as a meetup in San Francisco in 2012 has grown into a global sensation, drawing the likes of CEO Marc Benioff of Salesforce.com and US Chief Technology Officer Megan Smith to address software engineers, fintech managers, cybersecurity, healthcare, transportation, energy tech experts, database managers, IT systems and technology directors. Participants come to an annual affordable summit—just $199 for Early Bird registration—held in San Francisco and New York City. International Summits are hosted throughout the year with the amazing support of volunteers. The intention to bring in marginalized groups has driven Leanne Pittsford, CEO and Founder of Lesbians Who Tech, since inception.

"I started this as an experiment. I was pretty sure it would fail because my experience with the LGBTQ community was dominated by gay men. It was hard to get lesbian women to show up in high volume. The first moment we were all at the Castro Theater in San Francisco for the first summit, 2014, I call that Day One of being an organization. Before that it was really Happy Hours. The energy in that room was unprecedented," said Pittsford.

Currently, women make up 19 percent of the women in technology at Google (Google Diversity Report, Jan. 2016), a technology trendsetter in Silicon Valley. There are no formal statistics for lesbians in tech. So it's astounding that a former Equity and Social Justice Graduate with a master's degree from San Francisco State University could create a summit in NYC that boasted a roster of speakers comprised of 50 percent women of color and 100 percent queer women and their allies. One of the unique designs of Lesbians Who Tech summits is that presenters are allotted only ten minutes to get across their stories and ideas in TED-like talks. Their evening presentations are even shorter—five minutes. Not surprisingly, summits get rave reviews from attendees. And, there is ample time for "networking that doesn't suck" at cocktail hours and meetups geared to participants.

Early supporters of Lesbians Who Tech were surprised at the caliber and turnout at summits of an organization with the tagline, *Queer/Inclusive/Badass*. Kara Swisher, former *Wall Street Journal* columnist in Silicon Valley covering All Things Digital, and author and founder of Recode, was an early supporter. Pittsford had met her and her-then wife, Megan Smith, a Google VP, while she was a database and development administrator at Equality California (ECQA), the foremost gay marriage nonprofit organization in the state. While at EQCA, Leanne Pittsford was part of a senior team that grew the budget for the organization from $5 million to $15 million. The Valedictorian of her small San Bernandino high school parlayed her social skills into social justice.

Even the well-connected in Silicon Valley crave the kind of community Lesbians Who Tech creates. No seat-saving, just a welcoming, "Sure, sit next to me," at events. Leanne asked Megan Smith to speak at a White House event she was organizing for LGBTQ technologists. It was there that Smith got recruited to become the US Chief Technology Officer. Another Lesbians Who Tech networking success story.

In 2016, there were two full-time employees at Lesbians Who Tech, Leanne and a full-time PR manager and a contracted PR professional. Pittsford plans to hire two more staff in 2017, making the PR position full-time and hiring someone to manage the Edie Windsor Scholarship, a technology development scholarship that provides 50 percent of the costs of coding workshops and boot camps of the scholarship winner's choice. Why just 50 percent? Leanne is a firm believer that you're more invested when you share in the costs of your own education.

Another program that Leanne wants to "fade up" in 2017 is a Take a Lesbian to Work Day. This is a mash-up of Take Your Child to Work Days popular in Silicon Valley and mentoring programs for lesbians in tech, which are virtually nonexistent. Pittsford envisions a great deal of peer mentoring and ally mentoring in this informal, fun way of introducing lesbians to technology and technology to lesbians. If Marc Benioff, CEO of Salesforce.com, is any indication, when Kara Swisher asked him to come to the SF Lesbians Who Tech Summit in 2014, he replied, "One thousand lesbians who tech. You don't have to ask twice."

It is well-known that tech companies are predominantly white and Asian, young and male. Companies like Google and Facebook struggle to diversify their ranks. Google's numbers are abysmal, as outlined on its own diversity page.. Google's male employees comprise 69 percent of the workforce; 59 percent of the total workforce is white; 32 percent Asian; 3 percent Hispanic; and 2 percent African-American. Further, tech jobs are even more shocking, with only 19 percent of tech workers female, 57 percent white,

37 percent Asian, 3 percent Hispanic, and 1 percent Black (Google Diversity Report, 2016).

Pittsford's trajectory to becoming a thought leader in technology and diversity did not come without major hurdles. When Leanne's only brother and sibling was twenty-five, he died of undiagnosed cardiomyopathy and Leanne found her beloved brother, Tim, dead in his apartment. That's when she and her then-partner, Leah, decided to pack up and travel the world for eight months.

Pittsford considers herself a natural entrepreneur. She sees a hole in the marketplace and fills it. She never imagined she would find "doing good" via business, technology, and entrepreneurship. When Pittsford's brother died, he left her his life insurance policy of $100,000, an enormous sum when you're a renter in San Francisco and aged thirty-two. Instead of having fun, Pittsford invested the entire amount in a friend's fledgling software company. The company went belly-up and Pittsford lost all the money, but never lost the lessons she learned about the importance of supporting women and lesbians in technology and assessing risk/reward astutely. She continues to invest today.

Like any true entrepreneur, Pittsford is willing to take risks. At age thirty-five, Leanne Pittsford is on top of the world, a world she never knew was possible for her growing up in Hesperia, California. Because of her work, Pittsford got to meet eighty-seven-year-old Edie Windsor, the first person in New York City to own an IBM PC and one of the first senior software programmers at IBM. Windsor is legendary in the LGBTQ community for her successful *Windsor v.*

US Supreme Court case seeking to overturn the Defense of Marriage Act. Windsor and her wife, Thea Spyer, married in Canada at a time when gay marriage wasn't legal in New York. Spyer suffered from MS for years. The couple was together forty-one years. When Spyer died, the State of New York demanded that Edie Windsor pay $363,053 in estate taxes, as their marriage was not recognized. Windsor took her case to the Supreme Court and won recognition of her marriage, while taking a stand against and defeating the Defense of Marriage Act that used to make marriage possible only between a man and a woman in the US, on June 26, 2013.

Pittsford "loves risk and loves learning. Every failure is a lesson learned. I really learn by doing. A lot of people think of the negatives of risk taking—what you can lose—but the reality is that there's so much more to gain generally."

Her current partner, Pia Carusone, owns a distillery. They're doing vodka now, but soon will launch bourbon and rye. Carusone got her start in politics when she was the former Chief of Staff of the Arizona Congresswoman Gabby Gifford, who was shot and severely head-injured. Carusone helped the Gifford's launch their Super Pac to find a responsible gun solution. Pia lives in Washington, DC, and Leanne and Pia travel cross-country often, not letting many weeks go by without seeing one another in person. Technology closes the gap, with FaceTime and Skype calls in-between trips. Leanne's dachshunds, Sauce and Magoo, travel with her whenever she can take them. The dogs even have European passports!

Pittsford's latest brainchild is developing a pipeline of lesbians of color in tech. Her own story informs her outreach. She was very talented in math, but as a people person was not pushed into math. Her tests and scores were a fit for computer science, but there was no encouragement for her to go in that direction. Science, Technology, Engineering and Math—STEM education—has to start younger and reach broader swaths of the population. There's a strong need to educate tech companies to hire "developable talent" and train underrepresented populations to excel in technology. Coding boot camps, online education, non-traditional sources of talent are only some ideas to reach more people. "We believe this could be a game changer," Leanne said.

Currently, the majority of Lesbians Who Tech has two to eleven years of experience, putting them in the twenty-four to thirty-three age range. This is the generation that sees women role models in engineering, science, technology

"Take risks and look at the potential gains, not the potential losses. There's so much more to gain by risking. Even if you lose, you learn. And, SHOW UP. Many lesbians don't go out and meet other lesbians face-to-face for meetups, events and political causes. It's important to be there in person for other lesbians, your community and yourself."

Leanne Pittsford

and math, albeit few of them. This is a generation whose mothers, generally, worked. So, this is a group that is young, eager to learn, and eager to advance their careers. Lesbians Who Tech gives them an avenue for meeting like-minded professionals. Now, at last, they're not the only women in the room, let alone the only lesbians.

Her advice to young queer tech professionals: "Take risks and look at the potential gains, not the potential losses. There's so much more to gain by risking. Even if you lose, you learn. And, SHOW UP. Many lesbians don't go out and meet other lesbians face-to-face for meetups, events and political causes. It's important to be there in person for other lesbians, your community and yourself."

Robbie Tristan Szelei:
From Neo-Nazi Hit List in Hungary to US Citizen

Hungarian World Champion Ballroom, Latin and Show Dancer
NYC Same-Sex Ballroom Dance Teacher
Director of Digital and Social Media, VGD, NYC;
Clients Include: the City of New York; CUNY

One afternoon, walking with Robbie Tristan Szelei near his old stomping grounds in the Jewish Quarter, he startled me by saying, "One of the most dangerous people you could be with in Hungary is probably me." For two years, starting in 2007, Robbie was the producer of the Pride Parade and Mr. Gay Europe in Budapest. The right wing was getting stronger during poor economic times, from 2006-2007, and there were many protests against gays. This is the saddest story about Hungary. "We had twenty years of friendly, supportive gay pride parades. Although it was not okay to walk down the street holding your partner's hand, it wasn't violent or aggressive," Robbie explained. Unfortunately, in 2007, a radical group initiated major attacks against the Gay Pride Parade. People were very badly injured. Molotov cocktails were thrown at gay bars. Mr. Gay Europe, at the very last minute, had to move to a secret location because there was no guarantee of the security of gay men from all over Europe. Robbie Szelei, as the producer and organizer of these events, had both his name and address published on a neo-Nazi site as someone to focus on. At the time, Szelei felt like "a fearless pioneer." But he was scared when he heard the news. He talked to the police who were supportive. Because of the strong, yet small community, Szelei was not that afraid.

"Growing up under Communism, you had a longing for the West. But I think, being gay, there was an added level of that. The opportunities to live a fuller life as a gay man were obvious just 200 kilometers from our hometown in Vienna," he said. Szelei's longing for the West would be fulfilled when he moved to the US at age sixteen as an exchange student. He would stay in Long Island for 1.5

years. Though accepted to The Julliard School in musical and dance performance, Szelei could not afford to go. As a student from Hungary, the tuition and costs were out of the question. Ten years later, in 2005, Szelei came back to the States for the World Championship Ballroom Dance Competition in Sacramento, CA, with his dance partner from Hungary, Gergo Darabos. This duo was among the first, if not the only, same-sex ballroom dancers to win in Ballroom, Latin, and Show Dance. At the Gay Games in Chicago in 2006, Robbie and Gergo Darabos won Level A Gold in 10-Dance – all five Latin and five Ballroom categories -- Samba, Rumba, Cha-Cha, Jive, Paso Doble, Waltz, Tango, Quickstep, Foxtrot, and Viennese Waltz. In the 2010 Gay Games in Cologne, Robbie won Gold in Level B Latin with his student. Robbie began ballroom dancing in Hungary at age seven and quit competing at age fourteen, having become more interested in theater and musical performance. That interest served him well in the same-sex partner dancing world, which opened him up to a world of possibilities in the LGBTQ global community.

In 2006, Szelei organized a world championship contest for same-sex dancers in Budapest. However, it was the 50th anniversary of the 1956 Hungarian Uprising the very same week of the competition. There were demonstrations and violence. Molotov cocktails were thrown around the city center and dancers could not make it back to homes and hotels where they were staying. Dancers from the US and Europe glimpsed the terror of the right wing that week.

As Robbie tells it, "My life was changed forever for two reasons. One, when I started ballroom dancing at the age of seven, I learned and gained so much as a person. The discipline. The confidence to represent yourself in front of hundreds of people. The other major event was when I started to do same-sex dancing. That gave me strength as a gay man. And because of all of this with my teaching, I want to give back. I love seeing the same-sex couples discover this activity that they can do together and have fun, coming together and dancing and spending time together in a different way."

When Robbie and Gergo Darabos became successful with same-sex dancing, it was very new in the states. So the *NY Times*, the *LA Times*, and many media outlets were intrigued. Obviously, there was the sensational element of two men dancing together. "We actually had lots of offers to do reality TV shows. *America's Got Talent* wanted us to perform; at the time, I had to tell them I'm not American so that won't work. We were always very careful because we didn't know how it was going to be portrayed. It's very easy to show same-sex ballroom dancing as two gay clowns running around and doing something pansy or silly. We wanted only to help and build the community, not ruin it," he explained.

When Robbie arrived in Sacramento in 2007, he quickly organized Dancing in the River City, an annual same-sex ballroom competition and evening show that took place over Martin Luther King, Jr. holiday weekend (how fitting). His "partners in crime," the organizing committee— Cindy, Ellie, Lisa and Robert—held weekly gatherings. When Robbie put on shows, he forced everyone to participate. Robbie put everyone in '70s outfits and danced to a medley of Abba songs in the Sacramento Formation Team competition.

Dance is very intimate. There's no hiding with the body. That was no more evident when one of Robbie's students and a member of the organizing committee contracted cancer and had to have part of her quadriceps muscle removed. Robbie had to modify his teaching to adapt to his student's new challenge. There were more to come for his student: her cancer returned even more aggressively, and she finally had to have her leg amputated above the knee. Three years after leaving Sacramento for NYC, Robbie re-visited his student, in a wheelchair, and was inspired to see her fighting to choreograph a dance routine from her wheelchair. "I don't know too many people who would do this. She's such an inspiration, not just to me, but to the entire LGBTQ community," he said. Sadly, his star student, Cindy Mills, lost her battle with cancer and died in the Fall of 2016.

Robbie misses the *esprit de corps* of his mostly lesbian group of dancers in Sacramento. He so identified with them that he jokingly added that he even bought a Subaru Outback. He taught novices and beginners who not only got to participate in international competitions, but to travel with dancers from all over the world. For Robbie, teaching has always been about empowering people. While he wants them to dance as well as possible, it was more rewarding to give beginners a new set of skills or move them from novice to intermediate. From Robbie's perspective, there are already so many fantastic teachers who focus on the top dancers and few focusing on the novice dancer. "Until these days, I'd rather coach a wedding couple for their first dance than coach an A-Level competitive couple. It's just more rewarding. I think I'm also good at it. I'm good at making people comfortable in their skin while they are dancing," he explained.

Robbie, like most dancers and artists, has a day job now. He runs the digital advertising/social media department of a creative agency, working with clients like the City of New York. Even in his day job, he's a performer—presenting creative concepts or problem solving. "I think it's a common theme in my life. I like to find unique solutions for unique challenges," he said.

Robbie retired from dancing with Gergo Darabos in 2008 at age thirty. Since then, he's competed in Pro-Am with his students, in LGBTQ ballroom shows and events, and, most recently, the avant-garde Sean Dorsey's Fresh Meat Festival in San Francisco. The SF Bay Area audience is one Robbie delights in. Every year, the Fresh Meat Festival shows are sold out.

What's next? After striking out with at-risk NYC queer youth who showed more interest in having fun and hip-hop, Robbie is reaching out to SAGE, LGBTQ Seniors. They love the music of their youth and value ballroom dancing. He would also like to help people with depression through dance. He teaches mostly gay men and lesbians in NYC once a week. "Gay boys are more extroverted and interested in Latin. With my lesbians, it's Ballroom and Argentine Tango. They like a bit more intimate environment. That's the main difference," he said.

Advice to LGBTQ citizens of the world? "Find your passion and do it. Experiment until you find your people. If you want to learn about yourself, your partner, your community and the globe, same-sex partner dancing is a great way to go. When I teach, I create an environment where you're free to experiment." Robbie would probably reiterate— "Experiment."

"Growing up under Communism, you had a longing for the West. But I think, being gay, there was an added level of that. The opportunities to live a fuller life as a gay man were obvious just 200 kilometers from our hometown in Vienna."

Robbie Tristan Szelei

Ardel Haefele-Thomas, PhD:
A World of Firsts

Chair, LGBT Studies, City College of San Francisco
Author, First Undergraduate Transgender Studies
Textbook in the World

"My biological family—we don't talk, because, you know, 'I'm goin' to hell.' Only one has reached out to me in thirty years and she's a lesbian." Ardel Thomas grew up in the heart of the South, raised by a family of born-again, Bible-thumping Baptists. They always felt like an alien. And not just because they were queer. At age four, they questioned their uncle's racist comments when Dr. Martin Luther King, Jr. was assassinated. They came out when they were nineteen, and their grandmother responded by praying over them in earnest.

Their affinity for the disenfranchised, evident in the LGBT Pride Graduation at City College of San Francisco (CCSF), where they are Chair of LGBT Studies, began young. Growing up a tomboy, Ardel didn't like wearing the frilly dresses of their Oklahoma childhood. They empathized most with what their mother thought "the family dunce," their Uncle Kenneth, a washing machine repair man, and their Aunt Lorita, a garment factory worker. In their own family, Haefele-Thomas saw how hard people struggled and knew, even as a child, that education was the way out. So, it came as no surprise when they presented the first LGBT Pride Graduation's highest honor to a formerly homeless heroin addict, a transgender student. That graduate of community college is now a straight-A student in Creative Writing at Columbia University.

Haefele-Thomas, an Aries, is all about FIRSTS. They were the first to come out as queer in their family. They started the first independent, free-standing LGBT Studies Department in the US, and the second in the world. They secured A.A. degree status for LGBT Studies in California—

the first in the country. And Dr. Ardel Haefele-Thomas, with contributions from Thatcher Combs, is writing the first *Introduction to Transgender Studies* undergraduate textbook in the world, published by Columbia University's Harrington Park Press in 2017.

"I don't identify as Lesbian. This is going to put the interview off the rails. I've always preferred the word, *Queer*," she said. On a personal level, Haefele-Thomas wanted to look at transgender issues. They chose not to transition, though they've considered it for twenty years. "I actually identify as non-binary and use the pronoun, they, not she."

Dr. Haefele-Thomas presented for the second year in a row at the Transgender Archive Conference in Victoria, BC, Canada, in 2016. To them, "gender's a performance. It depends of the occasion." Their book is being piloted at Yale University, Penn State, and Colorado University-Boulder, where Haefele-Thomas finished their master's degree in English/Creative Writing and their bachelor's degree in women's studies, and at CCSF. "The response has been off the hook," they said. People are hungry for this book. People want this. While the book is theoretical, it is most of all, accessible. "Even my edgy, urbane, smart students in San Francisco and at Stanford often get gender and sexual orientation mixed up."

"My field of study at Stanford University was intersecting identities - gender, race, sexual orientation - reflected in 19th Century British Gothic literature, my other area of interest. I like to blame the Victorians for a lot of things. Gothic Horror of the late nineteenth century, post-1870, focused on people of dubious origins, gender and sexual identities."

Haefele-Thomas sees herself as both scholar and teacher. In an MSNBC interview, following the passage of California Senate Bill 48, the Fair, Accurate, Inclusive and Respectful (FAIR) Education Act, requiring persons with disabilities and lesbian, gay, bisexual, and transgender people be integrated into educational textbooks and the social studies curricula in California public schools by amending the California Education Code, Haefele-Thomas tells the story of their first day in Intro to LGBT Studies class. They often ask their globally diverse students in San Francisco, "Who has heard of Martin Luther King, Jr.?" and nearly all the hands go up, even those of newly minted students from China and El Salvador. However, when they ask, "Who has heard of Bayard Rustin?" inevitably, only one or two hands go up, and yet, Bayard Rustin was the chief strategist behind the 1963 March on Washington for Jobs and Freedom where Dr. Martin Luther King, Jr. delivered his famous "I Have a Dream" speech. African-American and openly gay, Rustin showed rare courage in the Civil Rights Movement in the US for which he was posthumously awarded the Presidential Medal of Freedom in 2013. His partner of ten years, Walter Naegle, accepted the award. As Haefele-Thomas asserts, LGBTQ history is buried so deep in the closet that even the most sophisticated urban students "are in the dark" about their own disenfranchised group's contributions to history.

"I'm fortunate. I teach the most edgy, diverse students in the world. At CCSF, at least forty-three languages are represented and, in any given class, five to ten students may be HIV-positive and two to five can be transgender. Often, at least one or two are homeless. By the time students sign up for my class, they've already come to terms with being queer. I share my own experience. I have an open door. My classes help students learn about queer history and queer culture, develop support networks and take pride in who they are "they develop their chosen families. As Armistead Maupin, a guest in my class, said, 'Do you want to belong to your biological family or your logical family?'"

Ardel Thomas married in October of 2008 in San Francisco, during the five month period when marriage was legal in California, to fellow English PhD graduate Lisa Haefele. Thomas and their wife changed their last names to Haefele-Thomas and went on to adopt a medically-fragile, African-American boy named Jalen. In his short life of eight years, Jalen has undergone three major heart surgeries. He was born with hypoplastic left heart syndrome. Hypoplastic left heart syndrome occurs when parts of the left side of the heart (mitral valve, left ventricle, aortic valve, and aorta) do not develop completely. The condition is present at birth (congenital). Surgery offers the best hope of survival. Currently, Jalen is a thriving second grader who depends on a wheelchair for long distances and uses an iPad to assist him with his fine motor skills, including writing, some of which were diminished due to complications from his prior heart surgeries. The right side of Jalen's body was underdeveloped. This has led the Haefele-Thomas's to become advocates for the differently-abled in Berkeley public schools and in the healthcare system. They advocate not only for their own child, but for those students whose families are unable to advocate for them. As the daughter of a doctor, Haefele-Thomas knows the medical jargon and their wife, as a government employee, understands the workings of bureaucracies. It has been and continues to be a challenge in their lives. Yet, "day-to-day, Jalen is a joy to be around. We didn't go through a period of grief that many biological parents go through when they find out their child is differently-abled. We knew, as much as you can know, going into it what we were getting into in adopting Jalen."

What does Jalen call Ardel? At home, "it's pop-pop or mom-mom. Jalen's teachers think Jalen is confused about gender, when in fact, he has a leg up on them. He himself is gender fluid. Somedays, he's our son. Other days, he's our daughter. He came up with a new category of gender identity, GROWN-UP!"

Beyond her own family story, Haefele-Thomas acknowledges that there are still many pressing issues for LGBTQ people in the US. Legal marriage is a start, but employment and housing discrimination still exist. Legal protections don't guarantee social protections or inclusion. School bullying is a deadly and pervasive problem. Gay/trans phobia and discrimination are still rampant among medical providers. Families still reject their LGBTQ sons and daughters, leading to one of the highest rates of suicide and homelessness of any population.

So how do LGBTQ youth build that necessary social support system? Taking classes and workshops with fellow LGBTQ students is one way. Joining LGBTQ clubs and organizations is another. Haefele-Thomas supports many LGBTQ advocacy groups, including National Center for Lesbian Rights: "They get it. It's about gender rights." They also support Frameline, a nonprofit dedicated to changing the world through the power of queer cinema, by purchasing films themselves at the institutional rate to share with their classes. They like the Queer Women of Color Media Arts Project, the Transgender Film Festival, and Sean Dorsey's Fresh Meat Productions.

Since 1998, Haefele-Thomas has participated in a variety of sports at the Gay Games, an international LGBTQ sporting competition that occurs every four years. In 1998, in Amsterdam, and again in 2002, in Sydney, Haefele-Thomas competed in powerlifting and took home gold medals. In 2006, in Chicago, Haefele-Thomas participated in both the swimming and ballroom dancing competitions. The Gay Games are for LGBTQ athletes and non-athletes alike, and are based on the principles of: "Participation. Inclusion. Personal Best."

Currently, Ardel and their wife, Lisa, take weekly Latin ballroom dance classes from a queer Latin ballroom dance champion. "It's a joy and a lot of fun for Lisa and me to dance. It's a great place for us to go and not be parents for an hour and to be together. And the LGBTQ dance community is a great way for us to get out and get to know people. LGBTQ people need safe spaces to socialize. We live in a heteronormative world most of the time. It's great to go into spaces where LGBTQ people are celebrated, not merely tolerated," they said.

What advice would Dr. Haefele-Thomas give to LGBTQ youth? "More than anything, be yourself. Demand to be equal. Seek out support from LGBTQ mentors and allies, friends and fellow travelers."

"LGBTQ people need safe spaces to socialize. We live in a heteronormative world most of the time. It's great to go into spaces where LGBTQ people are celebrated, not merely tolerated."

Dr. Ardel Haefele-Thomas

Louisa Wall: Marriage Speaks an International Language

Iwi : Ngāti Tūwharetoa, Hineuru, Waikato Tribunal Affiliations
Māori MP, Labour Party, Manuwera, Auckland, NZ
Sponsor of the Marriage Amendment Bill
NZ Silver Fern, Netball, 1989-92
NZ Black Fern, Rugby, 1994-2002
Gold, World Cup Champions, Rugby, 1998
New Zealand Rugby Women's Player of the Year, 1997

Louisa Wall became one of the youngest members of the New Zealand Parliament at age thirty-six. Born in 1972 in Taupo, New Zealand to a proud Māori family, her father was her hero and role model. Leslie Wall was chairman of the local Waitahanui *marae*, sacred communal gathering place, for thirty years. He showed her how to create a sense of community.

Louisa's father instilled in his eldest of four children the belief that she could do anything. She became a member of the New Zealand national netball team, the Silver Ferns, at the young age of seventeen. Her coach, Lyn Parker, convinced her parents that Wall would develop physically on the court with two two-hour-a-day practices and intellectually with her course of study, a sport and recreation qualification in Waikato. Eventually, Wall added to this two-year diploma in sport and recreation with a Bachelor of Social Policy and Social Work and a Master of Philosophy Social Policy from Massey University. Along the way, she switched from netball to rugby at age twenty-one; she lost passion for netball, realizing it was somewhat homophobic at that time, while Wall was just beginning to realize that she was a lesbian and found role models in rugby and within the Black Ferns, the New Zealand national rugby team. There she would excel, becoming New Zealand's Woman Rugby Player of the Year in 1997 and winner, as a member of the Black Ferns, of the Rugby World Cup in 1998. She played four years for the Silver Ferns and seven years for the Black Ferns.

"When I came out at age twenty-one, my beloved Dad worried I would be discriminated against and my Mum worried she wouldn't have *mokopuna*. Once my brother had a child, that worry went away. There were other lesbians playing rugby and within the Black Ferns, there was a critical mass so we were able to support one another. I had a strong sense of self pride, so whether people liked me or not, I let my play on the field speak for me and my sexual orientation was irrelevant to my performance."

Louisa Wall met her civil union partner in 2007 while they were both members of the Waiatarau branch of the Māori Women's Welfare League, which Prue Tamatekapua now leads as President of the national organization. Despite a fourteen-year age difference and the fact that Prue was the mother of two teenagers from a prior marriage, the couple fell in love. The two women found they shared common values as proud indigenous people of New Zealand: community, collective action, and strong *whanau*, extended family. "Our identity as indigenous people of *Aotearoa* means we are connected to the land, its mountains and its waters," Wall explained. "We are never alone, but part of a greater whole. We have a saying in Māori, 'Ehara taku toa I te toa takitahi - engari he toa takitini ke! My strength/being is not that of one person - but of thousands!" Louisa Wall wears a big, bold *Manaia* around her neck to remind her that her ancestors are always there as guardians.

After working in the health field, Wall saw the need for system changes and was attracted to the Labour Party, then led by Helen Clark, with the values of collectivism and equality of outcome. When asked what that meant, Wall said, without hesitation, "A stable home. When you come from a stable home with parents who are supportive you are able to go to work, attend school and to get a good education. Then you are in a position to control your own destiny." The Manurewa Electorate in South Auckland that Wall represents is diverse and issues of poverty and inequality are daily challenges. Less than half of the area's citizens own their own homes and many are working poor, unable to afford rent. Across Auckland, nearly 3,000 families are on the waiting list for government housing. The local Manurewa *marae* has set up a housing shelter for homeless families and has become a nexus for volunteerism. Education, as Wall well knows, is the way out of poverty and into a position of home stability and ownership. These issues present ongoing challenges for the Labour MP.

As a government representative, Wall's job is never really done. She spends three to four days a week in Wellington, taking the one-hour flight from Auckland to Wellington and back, thirty-two weeks of the year. Back home in her Manurewa electorate, Wall attends everything from school celebrations and events, community meetings, cultural events, church events, sports events, and many Māori, Pacific and Indian celebrations.

One of her biggest challenges today in Parliament, at age forty-four, is keeping fit. When she was playing international sports, she could eat whatever she liked and stay fit. Carb-loading, with mainly bread-based food before and after training, was compulsory. She tried giving up bread and sweets, but found it nearly impossible. So, she did what she's always done, upped her exercise routine. Her sister gave her a Fitbit, a not-so-subtle hint, a couple of years ago, and she's up to 12-14,000 steps a day. Wall is co-captain of a Parliamentary netball team, and seriously prepared for an inter-country Parliament match against the Federal Parliament of Australia in October 2016. She and her wife, Prue, try to walk an hour every morning. But, it's still a challenge.

Louisa Wall marries Prue Tametekapua, December 2015

Stylist and Photography by Taaniko and Vienna Nordstrom

Equality, fairness, commitment to fundamental human
rights, and a belief that all are born free and equal in
dignity and rights provides the platform for Wall's work.
This inspired her to take a lead role in the sponsorship
of the Marriage Amendment Bill which her partner,
lawyer Prue Kapua, helped her write. The effort to pass
the Marriage Amendment Bill began in 2011 and required
the same qualities that winning a World Cup required:
"Preparation. Dedication. Commitment over a long period
of time. Teamwork: we had to work together, Labour,
National, the Greens and other Members of Parliament
to achieve this goal," Wall said. The bill drew 21,533
public submissions, more than any other bill. Wall was
responsible for answering any questions. Most of those
discussions were conducted face-to-face, with Members
of Parliament, religious groups, youth groups, schools and
universities, and other interested groups and individuals.
There was a backlash against passage of the bill. Within
her Manurewa electorate, thirty-two religious leaders signed
a letter encouraging Wall to vote against her own bill. Some
detractors, like Family First, a fundamentalist Christian
lobby group in New Zealand, and the National Party
candidate, highlighted that Wall was a lesbian and that it
was Wall's Marriage Equality legislation, and even went
door-to-door in Louisa Wall's Manurewa electorate to make
sure everyone knew. However, she was re-elected by a clear
majority and her actions did not adversely affect the Labour
Party vote, her chief concern.

Wall was particularly proud of the level of discussion
during the debates: "We are a small nation. We rely on
one another. Our moral ethos as a country is to help those

in need. We automatically extend the hand of support
and friendship. We are a collaborative society. We have a
strong tradition of human rights—we were the first country
in the world to grant women the right to vote in 1893 and
the first to introduce an eight-hour workday in 1899." For
Louisa Wall, it was always a question of human rights.
"We conducted a respectful discussion, listening to all sides
and airing all the concerns across the NZ electorate in the
debates leading up to the third reading in Parliament,"
she said. Louisa Wall said the Marriage Amendment Bill,
which provided an opportunity for marriage between two
people, regardless of their sex, sexual orientation or gender
identity, and reinforced LGBTI (Lesbian, Gay, Bisexual,
Transgender, Intersex)—Queer is not a widely accepted term
in New Zealand—New Zealanders as equal citizens. She
made sure that this bill did not impinge on anyone's religious
freedom—no minister has to marry an LGBTI couple. The
Marriage Amendment Act grants equal adoption rights
to LGBTI married persons who by definition are spouses.
Under the Adoption Act 1955, only spouses can make a joint
application to adopt.

Passing the bill was like winning the World Cup in Rugby,
which she won as a member of the Black Ferns Rugby
Team in 1998. Wall now feels she has fulfilled her beloved
late father's legacy: "When you see injustice, do something
about it." When MP Louisa Wall's Marriage Amendment
Bill passed on the Third Reading on April 17, 2013, it made
New Zealand the thirteenth country in the world to legalize
same-sex marriage. As soon as the vote count was read,
77-Ayes, 44-Nos, the full gallery broke out in the *waiata,*
Pokarekare Ana, the Māori love song that most New

Zealanders learn at school. It was a reaction never before seen in Parliament.

"At the end of the day, Parliament did what New Zealand has always done—stood up for fundamental human rights, reinforcing that we are all born free and equal in dignity and rights," Wall said.

So, on December 18, 2015, MP Louisa Wall married "her darling Prue" Tamatekapua in Auckland on the five-year anniversary of their Civil Union. They didn't marry right after the passage of the bill because "it was never about us. It was about addressing discrimination perpetuated by the state against LGBTI citizens. That day was a special day. Now I can say that Prue is my wife. Prue and I were able to declare our love for one another. Marriage, after all, creates family and enables the use of wife or husband which speaks an international language."

The best part of Wall's job is making systemic change. When she was a social worker, she could help individuals, and this had little effect on society as a whole. In her role as MP, she meets with people from all walks of life and has the opportunity to make a lasting difference in society. "It's wonderful to see that New Zealand could have a global impact in legislating for marriage equality. We became part of a global conversation that was also taking place in the US, France, Ireland, and Australia," Wall said.

But not everyone's whanau is supportive of queer youth. Though Māori have always included takatapu in their indigenous identities, colonization and fundamentalist

Christian values have influenced some Māori communities, who find it hard to accept their takatapu and queer whānau. If young people have no family support, are bullied in school or are condemned from the pulpit, where do they turn? In a heteronormative world, LGBTI youth can turn to drugs, alcohol, and suicide because of the pain of isolation and rejection. "At minimum, the State has a responsibility within public institutions—government, schools, in public contexts—to ensure safety, fairness, and respect. The Education Review Office (ERO) has the responsibility to ensure that schools provide for the health and well-being of all our children. We are currently advocating for ERO to audit schools to ensure they are adequately providing for the health and well-being of LGBTI youth," explained Wall.

It's important to reach out to queer youth with positive images in schools, in sports, in the media, and throughout the community. All those in public spheres have

"Find the people—family, friends, teachers, coaches, counselors, pastors— who will support you and help you on your journey. There are helplines with people who can talk to you and who do care. Be proud of who you are. You are the potential of your ancestors and you are never alone."

Louisa Wall

a responsibility to communicate that being LGBTI is normal. What advice would Wall give to queer youth in New Zealand? "You are not alone. Find the people—family, friends, teachers, coaches, counselors, pastors—who will support you and help you on your journey. There are helplines with people who can talk to you and who do care. Be proud of who you are. You are the potential of your ancestors and you are never alone."

John "LongJones" Abdallah Wambere: Words That Scare You

Ugandan Activist in Asylum in the US
Appeared in Documentary *Call Me Kuchu*
Recipient of GLAAD Media Award, April 12, 2014
Introduced at GLAAD Media Awards Ceremony
by Kenyan Academy Award-winner Lupita Nyong'o

In February of 2014, John "LongJones" Abdallah Wambere was about to board a plane from Boston Logan International Airport headed home to Kampala, Uganda. Friends, family, and colleagues madly texted, emailed, and called him, warning him, "Do not come home. Do you want to be a martyr? They will kill you the moment you step off that plane in Uganda."

While LongJones, as he is affectionately known, was visiting friends in Boston, Uganda's President Yoweri Musveni signed the Anti-Homosexuality Act into law on Feb. 24, 2014. More than 30,000 Ugandans demonstrated in favor of the bill, originally introduced by MP David Bahati in 2009, making repeated homosexual offences punishable by death. The new bill carries with it an up-to life imprisonment for the crime of being homosexual *and* for aiding and abetting homosexuals. Helping disseminate sex education aimed at gays could be perceived as "aiding and abetting" homosexuals. In a country where more than 1.5 million Ugandans are living with HIV, this new law poses a major health crisis.

The World Bank, the UN High Commission on Human Rights, leaders of the US, UK, Australia, France, and Sweden, along with the European Parliament, condemned the bill and threatened to cut aid to Uganda. The Anglican Reverend Canon Gideon Byamugisha said that the bill "would become state-legislated genocide."

John Abdallah Wambere was not always gay. Some might say he was bisexual. After all, he had sex with a woman and he fathered a daughter, now sixteen: "I was not always gay. I struggled to live a straight life. It was really hard for

me. I locked myself in my room and cried and cried and cried.
I asked God to make me just like everybody else. To make
me straight. To make me attracted to women." Finally, out
of the pain of discrimination, out of isolation, out of a feeling
of bondage, Wambere refused to hide anymore. He had
already been outed by the Ugandan tabloid, *Red Pepper*, in
2005, beaten unconscious in 2009, and accused, even by his
own sisters, of having fifty child molestation cases against
him. Somehow, in Uganda, child molestation, the purview of
predominantly heterosexual men, is linked to homosexuals.
"Would I be walking the streets of Kampala if I had fifty
cases of child molestation against me?" Wambere asked.

The link was made and reinforced by American
Evangelicals who exported their "homosexuality is an
abomination," "homosexuals want to recruit your children,"
"homosexuals deserve to die," "homosexuals are pedophiles,"
to Uganda. Under the direction of anti-gay Massachusetts
pastor Scott Lively, American Evangelicals began their
campaign of hate against homosexuals in Uganda ten
years ago. The Sexual Minorities Uganda (SMUG)
nonprofit is bringing a suit against Lively for his role in the
persecution of LGBTI people in Uganda. The federal lawsuit
was set for an oral hearing on Oct. 5, 2016, in Springfield,
Massachusetts. "The American Evangelicals played a very
big role in pushing their anti-gay agenda. They brought
the idea to Uganda that gays were recruiting children into
homosexuality. That was language not many people in
Uganda used. They knew homosexuals existed, but they
never had the idea that homosexuals corrupted children
until the American Evangelicals brought this idea to
Uganda. At the end of the day, lots of money was sent

down to Uganda from these churches to anti-gay groups," Wambere explained.

While many young gay activists reacted with anger and wanted to respond violently, Wambere, as an LGBTI activist in Uganda since the co-founding of Spectrum Ugandan Initiatives in 2002, a health education and advocacy group for LGBTI persons, felt it was his responsibility as a leader to encourage nonviolent action. Many cases have been won in court, and LongJones feels that a nonviolent approach holds the most hope for the LGBTI community in Uganda.

Along with the first out gay man in Uganda, teacher David Kato, LongJones agreed to appear in the documentary, *Call Me Kuchu*, a Swahili-Kenyan abbreviation of Makucho and code word in Uganda for gay. Directors Katherine Fairfax Wright and Malika Zouhali-Worrall began filming the everyday lives of LGBTI persons in Uganda in 2010. Wambere wanted to show that gay people were just like everyone else. They were responsible. They had jobs and homes. They had families and friends. They had the same humanity as everyone else.

In January of 2011, David Kato and Kasha Jacqueline Nabagesera brought suit against the Ugandan tabloid *Rolling Stone* (no relation to the US publication), which had published the names, home and work addresses and phone numbers and photographs outing many homosexuals in Uganda with the headline, "Hang Them!" The two won a landmark victory in the High Court. But two months later, David Kato was bludgeoned to death with a hammer in his own home. After that, LongJones feared for his life. "After they killed David Kato, I saw that these were not mere words, but that they meant to inflict pain on me to the extent of murder. I mean hearing someone openly say you deserve to die, you should be killed. I mean, these are words that scare you," said LongJones.

John "LongJones" Abdallah Wambere and Academy Award-winner, Kenyan Lupita Nyong'o, GLAAD Media Awards for Call Me Kuchu, 2014 www.glaad.org.

Photo by Andrew H. Walker

With so much going on and the film about to be released
in 2012, Wambere had an epiphany. Wambere stood tall
and not only appeared in the documentary, but promoted
it. "Come what may, let it be. In a sense, there was so much
fear, that I surrendered all that fear after the film," he said.
In promoting the film around the world, Wambere found
a warm reception. The film won thirteen international
awards, including the 2014 GLAAD Media Award for Best
Documentary. So, in April 2014, in front of a predominantly
Hollywood audience, John "LongJones" Abdallah Wambere,
in a stylish tuxedo given to him by the producers, accepted
the award from Academy Award-winning Kenyan actress,
Lupita Nyong'o, who said, "I stand in solidarity with those
fighting for an accepting and just world." Wambere spoke
for his LGBTI activists still in Uganda who have been
kidnapped, tortured, and jailed. HIV clinics were raided.
LGBTI activists were "devastated, not defeated" by the bill's
passage. It cost Wambere his country, his family, his friends,
his home, his job and his partner. The Hollywood audience
gave him a standing ovation.

When Wambere applied for asylum with the help
of Boston's GLAD legal team, he had to surrender his
passport and was stateless for nine months. In November
of 2014, Wambere was granted asylum and given work
authorization. He returned to the travel industry in Boston,
but wended his way to a nonprofit group dedicated to
helping victims of domestic violence. He misses his country
terribly, the community, the gossiping sessions calling one
another "ladies" and talking in his own language deep into
the night. He misses walking the streets of Kampala, the
mountains, the lakes, and the smells of "home." He misses

family and friends. In 2016, he applied to bring his daughter
to the US and her mother agreed. In her heart, the mother
must know that this place would offer her daughter more
opportunity. Weirdly enough, most of all, he misses the
green bananas, *matoke*, of his homeland. These bananas
are mashed and fried, prepared like Irish potatoes, back
home in Uganda. A friend brought him some and he could
hardly bear to eat them. He wanted to hold on to the green
bananas for as long as he could, as though by doing so, he
could hold on to the Ugandan home he had to give up.

And, yes, the black tuxedo with the satin lining, is still
hanging in John LongJones Abdallah Wambere's closet,
waiting for the next gala fundraiser for his beloved LGBTI
community in Africa. Just last week, he raised money in
Boston for LGBTI refugees in Kenya. And, perhaps, his
partner of five years, a closeted gay man in Uganda, will
put a ring on John's finger. "Thanks, someday, we will be
married. I can't wait for the day he comes and puts the ring
on my finger. Oh, Kathleen, I cannot wait for that day!"

Wambere has some unusual advice for young queer
Ugandans: "My advice would be for those who haven't
come out to their families, let them get their education first.
Don't provoke. It may sound mean because we all want
the freedom to be who we are, but if you are not ready to
set out in the world on your own, DO NOT COME OUT
TO YOUR FAMILY. Keep a low profile until your family
has finished supporting you to get your education. If your
family cuts support for your education, you're nobody out
in the community. That's why so many LGBTI Ugandans
are illiterate and, thus, powerless. Be conscious in a country

"Keep a low profile until your family has finished supporting you to get your education. If your family cuts support for your education, you're nobody out in the community. That's why so many LGBTI Ugandans are illiterate and, thus, powerless. Be conscious in a country where you are discriminated against... Don't be pressured by family into an unhappy marriage. Be mindful of your personal security."

John "LongJones" Abdallah Wambere

where you are discriminated against. Complete your education. Research health issues and gay men. Don't be pressured by family into an unhappy marriage. Be mindful of your personal security."

Mindful of his own personal security, John LongJones Abdallah Wambere made the ultimate sacrifice. Safe in asylum in the Boston-area of the United States, Wambere continues to advocate for the rights of LGBTI Ugandans and LGBTI persons throughout Africa.

Rick Welts: Breaking the Sports Ceiling

President and COO, Golden State Warriors
Highest-Ranking Professional Men's Sports Team
Executive to Come Out
(Dan Barry, *New York Times*, May 15, 2011)
2016 Recipient of Anti-Defamation League
Torch of Liberty Award
2015 National Basketball Association (NBA) Champions
2015 Sports Team of the Year (*Sports Business Daily*, May 2016)
2015 San Francisco PRIDE March celebrity Grand Marshal

He knew he was gay from a young age, but he didn't come out publicly until he was fifty-eight. There were no role models in men's professional team sports in the executive suite and he's still the only one who is openly gay in early 2017. Rick Welts grew up in Seattle, WA with a passion for sports. He and his father, also University of Washington alum, went to Seattle SuperSonics games together and connected around sports. So it was not surprising that Rick secured a position as ball boy with the Sonics when he was sixteen. All the while, Rick kept putting himself on a two-year plan—*if I feel this way in two years, then I'll worry about those feelings then*. At the end of every two years, he added two more. For the boy in the suburbs, he didn't want to be gay. A furtive note in high school to a family minister didn't change the environment of heteronormative pressure one iota.

Rick followed his professional dream of working in the NBA. While at the Sonics, he was affectionately the "white boy" at the end of the hall to his boss, Bill Russell.. Russell was a legend who had eleven NBA Championship rings in his collection and was coach of the Sonics from 1973-1977. Welts promoted the Sonics as its PR person when it won one of its first championships in 1979.

Welts' marketing wizardry led him to the league office in New York City where, working with Commissioner David Stern for the next seventeen years, he was instrumental in pulling off the marketing coup of the sports world, convincing FIBA and the ABA to allow the USA to compete in the Olympics with professional basketball players as other countries had been doing since inception. The Dream Team—Michael Jordan, Scottie Pippen, Magic Johnson, Larry

Bird, Chris Mullin, Charles Barkley, Patrick Ewing, and others—swept the field by margins of forty-four in all but the Croatia contest, and won the Gold Medal in Barcelona in 1992. As Chief Marketing Officer, working with NBA attorney, Val Ackerman, Welts helped to launch the successful Women's National Basketball Association. The two received the prestigious *Brandweek* Marketer of the Year Award in 1998 for the feat. Prior attempts at creating a professional women's basketball league had failed, yet this one is going strong twenty years later.

While at the NBA League offices in New York, Welts' first partner of fourteen years, Arnie Chinn, died of AIDS. Rick took just two days off, telling David Stern that he just lost "his best friend." When Welts returned to the office, he awaited HIV test results without telling anyone the true story. That week was a very lonely one for the men's team sports executive, who kept his personal and his professional life separate. Fortunately, Welts was HIV-negative, but the grief over the death of his partner he had to bear in silence at work.

His next fourteen-year relationship ended in part over Rick's closeted life at work. The discomfort of not being able to include his partner in work parties and events was wearing. Rick's partner didn't want to be invisible. That relationship ended in 2009.

Welts served as president and CEO of the Phoenix Suns from 2002-2011. After much soul searching and consulting some of the best minds in media strategy, Welts decided to come out in the media. He had been OUT to friends and family in his adult life and had a great support network. He consulted his mother, who'd known Rick was gay his entire adult life, to ensure that he would not embarrass or upset the family. She gave Rick her full blessing as she lay dying with lung cancer. Unfortunately, she died before the story came out.

The media strategists suggested Rick Welts, a relative nobody to the public as most sports executives are, tell his story through some of the biggest names in sports—players, coaches, and commissioners Welts had worked with throughout his very successful career. One of the first people he approached was Bill Russell. Meeting at his home in Washington, Rick came into Bill's study and was confronted by a photo of Barack Obama and Bill Russell, awarded a Presidential Medal, with the inscription, "*You are my inspiration.*" Pretty intimidating for what Welts was about to ask—that Bill be willing to talk to *New York Times* Pulitzer Prize-winning journalist, Dan Barry. Russell was never a fan of media interviews, but he didn't hesitate to make himself available. David Stern, NBA Commissioner, gave Welts the first bear hug in their thirty-year association when Welts met with him to share his decision to go public and to articulate that he was gay for the first time. Val Ackerman supported him wholeheartedly, as did Phoenix Suns superstar Steve Nash. When the story broke on the front page of the *NY Times* on May 15, 2011, Rick Welts was not quite prepared for the outpouring of support from around the country.

"I signed up for this. I wasn't prepared to do this earlier in my career. Fortunately, I've learned that I'm successful because of who I am, not in spite of who I am," he said. The world of sports would agree. As soon as Welts left the Phoenix Suns to re-locate to California to be nearer his partner, Todd Gage, of Sacramento, the offers came pouring in. It was when Joe Lacob and Peter Guber of the Golden State Warriors called that Rick answered just three weeks after leaving the Suns.

Rick Welts, President and COO, Golden State Warriors, 2015 NBA Champions, with partner, Todd Gage, Southwest Airlines VP; Grand Marshal at 2015 San Francisco Gay Pride Parade

Photo by Josh Edelson

After a six-hour meeting at Lacob's home in Atherton, Welts and the Golden State Warriors ownership agreed on the vision for the sports franchise. Lacob was about winning and giving the organization the resources to do that. Together, the ownership welcomed diversity—diversity of perspectives and diversity across race, gender, sexual orientation, and age. Unlike many owners, the Warriors' owners, veterans of Silicon Valley and Hollywood, wanted to hear different opinions at the table. Today, the Warriors boast one of the most diverse teams at the highest levels of the organization.

Finally, Welts could be fully his authentic self at work. He met Todd Gage at the top of a stairway to a Southwest Airlines flight to Phoenix. "Blame it on the Burbank Airport," he joked. They still had the roll up stairs on the tarmac. Flight attendant Todd made quite an impression on Welts. At the end of the one-hour flight to Phoenix, Rick handed Todd a napkin with his name and phone number handwritten on it. It would take a full year before they would get together. Todd was afraid that someone with such a high profile as a sports executive would be too high-maintenance for him and his life as a dad in Sacramento.

After some convincing, Rick got together with Todd and they've been together ever since. Todd has gone through the coming out process with Rick, and that only strengthened their bond. Rick lives with Todd in San Francisco and Sacramento so Todd can share custody of his two kids, a fifteen-year-old girl and a twelve-year-old boy, on Thursday through Saturday nights in Sacramento. So, whenever Rick's not away for a basketball game, Rick hops on Amtrak at Jack London Square in Oakland on a Friday and heads up to Sacramento to be with the family for the weekend. "It's not something I expected at this time in my life, but I cherish every moment of it," he said.

Unlike all those lonely years when Rick begged off social engagements or came to team parties alone, Rick brings Todd Gage everywhere with him to Warriors events. The owners, staff, coaches, and players all welcome Todd's presence. Todd has said he's at so many Warriors events that he "should be on the Warriors payroll."

Todd keeps track of all the complications of their schedules—two houses, two kids, two dogs, two careers. Todd is the first VP of the union of 14,000 flight attendants for Southwest Airlines, based in Dallas, TX.

As Rick Welts has found out, his coming out has led to unexpected benefits. His partner's life as a dad in Sacramento made it easier for Rick Welts to navigate the State politics that helped teams and businesses lobby for AB 900, a bill that limits litigation for projects of great importance to the state and that meet the highest sustainability standards to nine months. The passage of that bill paved the way for the Apple campus in Cupertino and the new Warriors-owned San Francisco Arena at Mission Bay in San Francisco. On track for a 2019 opening, the 18,000-seat sports and entertainment arena will be one of Welts' biggest achievements yet.

Following the 2015 NBA Championship season and the 2016 NBA Finals, losing to Cleveland in the seventh game after setting the best-ever regular season record of 73-9, the

Warriors are on top of the Western Conference in 2016-2017. "The dream of all the things we had hoped for six years ago when we met have come true. I pinch myself every day that I get to do what only thirty other people in the country get to do—come to work every day working for an NBA team that exemplifies the excellence I aspire to. While it's great, it doesn't indicate a finish line. We have an opportunity to build one of the great franchises in sports. You do that over time. We're focused on creating a unique environment that allows everyone the courage to fail, but not to make the same mistakes twice. We encourage different points of view at the table; we think that leads to better decisions. And, we hired a coach in Steve Kerr who had never coached an NBA team before, but who exhibited high potential and, more importantly, high character. That's what makes the Warriors unique," Welts said.

The Warriors influence extends beyond the court into the community. In 2015, the Warriors Community Foundation, of which Rick Welts is a Board member, donated $2.7 million with the mission of helping underserved children in the San Francisco Bay Area. The feeling is that when underrepresented minority kids get the positive attention and help they need early on, their chances for success improve dramatically. The Foundation has refurbished sixty outdoor basketball courts, given community grants in Oakland and San Francisco for educational and developmental programs, and hosted several free ticket school programs that bring young school kids in contact with Warriors basketball stars as positive role models.

Rick Welts is "cool under pressure," much like the Warriors coach Steve Kerr he's known since his Phoenix Suns days. But today, that pressure doesn't include hiding his sexual orientation at work. He can bring his entire authentic self to the Golden State Warriors offices in Oakland, California. As for all the student athletes who are passionate about sports and considering coming out, he has this to say: "What people forget is that most professional athletes are, by definition, twenty-somethings. They have a short window to be successful in their careers. They're part of the delicate chemistry of teams. So that chemistry, more than even coming out, can be affected by the media and fan attention a player gets if he or she comes out. There's no timeline or script for coming out. It's a very personal decision and a private journey. You'll come out when it's the right time for you. You'll know when it's that time." For Rick, it took nearly sixty years.

"There's no timeline or script for coming out. It's a very personal decision and a private journey. You'll come out when it's the right time for you. You'll know when it's that time."

Rick Welts

Claudia Brind-Woody:
IBM Trailblazer

VP and Managing Director for Global Intellectual
Property Licensing
IBM, United Kingdom
Former Graduate Assistant Coach under
Coach Pat Summitt, Tennessee
Fifth Most Powerful LGBT Executive in the World
(Business Insider, April 15, 2016)

When she was young and poor and sharing an apartment with Coach Pat Summitt of the Lady Vols at the University of Tennessee, Claudia Woody never thought she'd become one of the fifth most powerful LGBT executives in the world. Coach Summitt, the winningest basketball coach, men's or women's, in history, taught her to play to people's strengths and minimize their weaknesses. That's a management skill Claudia Brind-Woody uses every day in her role as VP and Managing Director of Global Intellectual Property Licensing for IBM.

"I thought my career was going to be in women's athletics at first. After coaching with Pat and having completed my master's degree, University of Tennessee wanted an athletics director in women's athletics. After doing that for a while, University of Texas came calling. I was the Assistant Women's Athletics Director there and ran the first Final Four for Women's Basketball that ever sold out," she said. That still doesn't explain Brind-Woody's path to IBM.

A classic overachiever, Brind-Woody got both an MBA and a JD degree and jumped fields to run the intersection between technology and sports for the Atlanta Olympics. The systems integration with IBM was extremely successful, so IBM recruited Woody to come work for them. Opportunities knocked and Claudia opened the doors. So for nearly twenty years, Claudia Brind-Woody has been an IBMer and can't stop gushing about the company. "I'm really proud to be an IBMer. In 1953, IBM had its first non-discrimination policy. Think about that "before the Civil Rights Act, before the Equal Pay Act, because leaders like CEOs Thomas Watson Sr. and Thomas Watson Jr. believed in those values. In 1984, we added sexual orientation. In 2000, we added gender identity and gender expression. IBM has enabled me to stand on a very powerful and well-known brand as one of the Co-Chairs of our global IBM LGBT Executive Task Force."

Kneeling Coach Pat Summitt, winningest coach, men's or women's NCAA Basketball, Claudia Woody (next to media table), Graduate Assistant Coach, University of Tennessee.

Photo by Claudia Woody's brother

So how long has Brind-Woody been out? Since B-school.
And it was Pat Summitt who encouraged her to be her
authentic self. Even while Pat was dating her future
husband, and while Claudia was dating a woman,
Summitt supported Claudia's equal right to be herself in
her relationships. That, along with a supportive father
and mother from a small factory town in Virginia, gave
Claudia the courage to be out her entire career. And, as she
points out, you're never just out and done with it. You're
constantly coming out—to a new team of employees, to a
new manager, to a new business partner, to a new client.
And is she out to her clients? Absolutely. Brind-Woody
doesn't feel she can be as effective as she is if she has to
hide who she is in her business dealings.

In 2011, Brind-Woody won the Out & Equal Trailblazer
Award and was listed in *GO* magazine as "100 Women
We Love." In 2012, she was included in *The Guardian's*
WorldPride Power List Top 100. The *Financial Times* named
Brind-Woody fifth on its "OUTstanding in Business 100
LGBT Role Models" in 2015.

All the awards and accolades tell only part of the story.
When Brind-Woody was representing IBM at the first
Euro Pride ever in a former communist country—Poland in
2010—she was urged by security to not march or to wear
an IBM t-shirt. But Brind-Woody asked herself, "If not me,
who? If I'm not willing to stand up for the folks in Poland
at a time when they're afraid to be out, who will be? If I'm
not courageous enough to take a stance and march, how can
I be genuine and authentic when I'm speaking in an air-
conditioned conference room about LGBTQ rights? I decided

to do something hard, a bit scary." And the hostile crowds lining the streets did throw eggs at the protestors and shout hateful slogans. But it was a moment of solidarity with queer people of the world still living in fear and under threat in their own societies, and it was a defining moment for Claudia and one she'll never forget.

In addition to her role as deal-maker for IBM, Brind-Woody plays the role of diversity coach and mentor to IBM teams. Her sports background comes to the fore when she approaches predominantly middle-aged white male groups and asks them who the most important player on the team is if the team wants to win. In America, they'll say quarterback or pitcher or point guard. In England, they'll say striker. It varies by sport and country. Then Brind-Woody will ask, if you have a team of all strikers and I have a team made up of strikers, goal keepers, midfielders, defenders, and fullbacks, who is going to win the soccer game? Inevitably, they'll say, Claudia with the diverse team will win every time. That's how she shows them with real-life examples close to their hearts why diversity is important. No PowerPoint presentation. No data-rich charts. Just a simple sports analogy everyone can relate to in their everyday lives.

Her coaching and sports background translates into behaviors that are effective in the business environment every single day. "The notion of the team game: it's understanding that people play different roles. It's not how many points I scored, but did the team win? When you help people understand that and you reward them for it, everybody gets a gold medal."

How did Claudia Brind-Woody react when she found out that Coach Pat Summitt was diagnosed with early-onset Alzheimer's disease? "It made me very sad and very proud of her. That was her last competition, that was the last foe that she had to battle with and she did it with courage and grace that I only hope to touch. Her willingness to be the face of a disease most people are too embarrassed to even talk about "talk about being OUT "now, that was inspiring!"

Being authentic and open has actually helped Claudia Brind-Woody win deals for IBM. In one negotiation, because she was open about being lesbian, two or three professionals on the other side of the table came out, and that affinity smoothed the discussions. In another big deal last quarter, when the team was living together and working sixteen hours a day, things would come up naturally in conversation during breaks. *Where are you from? Where do you live now? Are you married? Do you have kids?* In the ordinariness of being comfortable, saying, "My wife, Tracie, and I live in Oxfordshire, England. She's a banker with Deutsche Bank and we have two miniature greyhounds," she brokered conversations. It's that making queer just *ordinary* that allows everyone at the negotiating table to relax and be real.

So, since her early days as assistant coach to the great Coach Pat Summitt, Brind-Woody has been out. In her ordinary interactions, she feels LGBT professionals sometimes underestimate their straight colleagues and their ability to embrace "our common humanity. Part of it is just relaxing enough to give them the opportunity. So when I say, my wife Tracie and I went to Wyoming horseback riding, the conversation becomes more about the Wyoming vacation, horseback riding, and not that I have a wife."

There are three models of approaching diversity in global corporations:

Tracie and Claudia Brind-Woody (Right)
Marry in New York

Photo by Steven Rosen

1. **"When in Rome"**: in difficult countries, those corporations just do what the laws say to do;

2. **Embassy Model**: regardless of country, within the walls of IBM, IBM values of non-discrimination are adhered to. Employees are valued, welcomed, promoted and respected based on merit, not any other characteristic;

3. **Advocate Model**: if IBM goes into a country that does not protect LGBT citizens and has laws that discriminate, the company and its employees work to advocate for political and social change.

At a minimum, in every country, IBM follows the Embassy Model. Everyone within IBM is safe to be who they are. And in more and more countries, IBM plays an advocate role. For example, IBM has partnered with other global companies to run LGBT business forums in India. The HR system in India gave employees the option to identify as LGBT, and 1,000 Indian IBMers did. Another 1,000 self-identified as straight allies in India, in spite of laws outlawing homosexuality there. IBM has an LGBT Business Development Group that brings in about $50 million a year in regions of Asia, Europe, and West Africa. "If we assume our clients are straight, we're going to be wrong about 10 percent of the time, right?" Claudia asked.

One of Claudia's proudest moments as an IBM LGBT advocate was when she got to meet Edie Windsor. Windsor was one of the top technical women at IBM in the '50s, '60s and '70s. Windsor retired from IBM to become a full-time caregiver for her wife of forty years, Thea Speyer, who suffered from MS. When Speyer died in 2009, Windsor was slapped with $363,053 in federal estate taxes. In *US v. Windsor*, SCOTUS ruled in favor of Windsor in 2013, striking down the Defense of Marriage Act as unconstitutional. Now, Claudia and her British spouse, Tracie, can return to Claudia's Virginia farm if they like when they retire because of former IBMer Edie Windsor's courageous fight for equality.

Claudia Brind-Woody has two pieces of advice for LGBT professionals: "Have the courage to be yourself AND be very good at something. If you are, it won't matter if you're male or female, black or white, gay or straight. You'll be valued on your merit. Obviously, in some countries, you must be smart, circumspect and, above all, safe. It doesn't mean you can't claim who you are and value your authentic self. You don't have to contemplate suicide because you're surrounded by negative messages. If you work for a company that doesn't allow you

"Have the courage to be yourself AND be very good at something... You'll be valued on your merit. Obviously, in some countries, you must be smart, circumspect and, above all, safe."

Claudia Brind-Woody

to bring your whole self to work, you may want to look for a company like IBM that does, where the company is safe and supportive of being openly LGBTQ."

Everyday Heroes

1. **Petra and Stacy Barneveld-Taylor,** Stacy Taylor, Retired LAFD Battalion Chief and Co-Founder of LAFD Women in the Fire Service; Petra Barneveld, Lincolnshire Fire and Rescue Service, UK

2. **Katerina Blinova,** UC Berkeley Award-Winning Computer Scientist, Dolby Laboratories Senior Software Engineer, and Same-Sex Ballroom Dancer; Refugee from Uzbekistan

3. **Jose Comoda and Chris Phan,** First Southeast Asian Gay Games Latin Ballroom Dance Champions

4. **Jac Grandchamps and Valerie Sans**, Belgian and French Co-Founders of French Escapade

5. **Jim McSweeney,** Manager of UK's only LGBT bookstore, Gay's the Word, in London, since 1997

6. **Peggy Moore,** Statewide Political Director for Organizing for America, California's Political Director, Obama's 2012 Re-Election Campaign, and Senior Special Advisor for Mayor of Oakland, Political Consultant

7. **Andreas Ozzuna,** Argentinian Small Business Owner, Wooden Table Baking Co.

8. **Eric and Mat Rosswood,** Gay Co-Parents in Kansas; Eric is author of *Journey to Same-Sex Parenthood*

9. **Gloria Soliz, MDiv.,** Founder of The Last Drag Smoking Cessation Program since 1991 and Co-Founder of

Coalition of Lavender Americans on Smoking & Health;
Co-Chair of the Bethany United Methodist Church
Covenant Council

10. **Christina Yin,** Senior Programmer Analyst of California
Department of Healthcare Services and Member of
China Moon Dance Troupe; from Shanghai, China

Stacy Barneveld-Taylor and Petra Barneveld-Taylor: Out of the Fire

Stacy Taylor, Retired LAFD Battalion Chief and Founder/President of LAFD Women in the Fire Service, 1995-2012

Petra Barneveld, EMT and Firefighter, Lincolnshire Fire and Rescue Service

They became firefighters to save lives and serve the community. They were not prepared for the sexual harassment, gender discrimination, homophobia, and xenophobia they encountered.

For Petra Barneveld, who grew up in Tenerife, Spain, born to Dutch parents and went to British schools, the response in the 30,000-person town of Spalding in Lincolnshire in the East Midlands of the UK was, "You're not from around here, are you?" The xenophobia intensified during the 2015 Brexit vote. Many townspeople live insular lives, growing up, working, living, and dying in the small town of Spalding. When Petra first joined the Fire Brigade in London at age twenty-one, it was quite the opposite. In the melting pot of London, there was little time for xenophobia. When she re-joined the Fire and Rescue Service, she was thirty-four, and had to undergo the physical training all over again. When asked how she did it, she said, "Sheer stubbornness, I guess." That, and an interim job at Dr. Martens shoe factory lifting boxes and loading pallets.

Why did Petra Barneveld-Taylor, an EU citizen who spoke three languages fluently and two passably, held a computer science degree from the University of Kent in Canterbury, have such a hard time? In two words: gay marriage.

When Petra Barneveld first met Stacy Taylor at an international Women in the Fire Service conference in Colorado in 2003, it was the first time she was around so many lesbians. She wasn't sure of her sexual orientation, but she knew she liked Stacy as a friend. They continued their friendship through both their breakups as Petra had realized she was a lesbian and had, as she says, two very tragic relationships. On a whim, after many expensive international phone calls, Petra left London and surprised Stacy on her doorstep in LA. Flummoxed, all Stacy could say was, "I haven't even had a shower." She was in a track suit and studying for her captain's exam.

Stacy and Petra Barneveld-Taylor in Fire Turnouts.

Photo by Piper Denlinger

Petra, with London Fire Brigade's allocated leave, stayed twelve days. That was in November of 2006. In December, she invited Stacy to the well-regarded NY's Eve Concert in Vienna. Petra had purchased rehearsal tickets for December 28 for her ex, and now wanted to share the experience. Petra did so much more than that. With a dash of Dutch courage, she bought a placeholder titanium ring, brought a vial of glitter, sang, "Christmas Bride," got down on one knee and asked Stacy to marry her in a horse-drawn carriage in Vienna just as it started to snow.

What began as a friendship turned into romance, despite a 17-year age difference. Petra was not concerned about the age difference and had to assure Stacy that she was not going to trade her in for a younger model.

That was the beginning of a long and torturous road to being together. They had no idea how hard it was going to be just to find a way to be together. In 2007, Petra took a one-year career break, came to LA, and studied to become an Emergency Medical Technician. During that year, the two women of the fire service discovered they were, indeed, compatible. So, in 2008, Petra quit the London Fire Brigade, moved to California, and began studying nursing.

Though she performed well in school and Stacy did very well in her job, Petra "felt trapped in the States." She wasn't doing what she loved. Stacy was paying international tuition fees. Petra couldn't work according to immigration rules for those on student visas and barely could hold on. Finally, Petra suffered a severe identity crisis when, after successfully completing community college pre-reqs, she entered nursing school and discovered she hated it. She hated being cooped up inside all day and missed the excitement and freedom of being a firefighter. Petra made the tough decision to return to the UK in hopes of getting back into the Fire Service.

During the three more years apart, Stacy was promoted to Captain I, Captain II, and Battalion Chief. Petra was never present for one of her badge pinnings. That really hurt Stacy. Everyone else thanked wives and husbands, partners and children, and Stacy couldn't share those glorious moments with the most important person in her life. So, promotions for Stacy were "bittersweet." Fortunately, her twin brother came, but her parents had passed and she couldn't share those high points with the love of her life.

For Stacy, the road to acceptance with the Los Angeles Fire Department was fraught with sexism and homophobia. In her very first year, the captain of one station pulled her aside and said, "I know you're a lesbian. And, honestly, we don't want lesbians in our fire department." Stacy was still in her probationary year and very worried about his talk with her. Then, on the job, a drunk broke a beer bottle and came at a crowd and Stacy subdued him with some martial arts techniques she'd learned off-duty. Now that same captain nicknamed Stacy his "dyke fire bitch," as some badge of honor. At another probationary station, a fellow firefighter kept "hitting on her" despite her telling him she was gay and despite the fact that he was already in another relationship. As co-founder of LAFD Women in the Fire Service, Stacy took lots of ribbing and harassment on the job. Fortunately, she had entered LAFD at age twenty-nine, after having been a record producer and a chef. Those chef skills won her many friends and allies as cooking skills represent high art in fire stations.

While Stacy would never say she saved a life—she'd leave that to the doctors and ER nurses—she did remember

Petra Barneveld-Taylor with Lincolnshire
Fire and Rescue
Photo by Stacy Barneveld-Taylor

changing a life. She met a young girl in West Hollywood named Alex who'd just been T-boned in a car-motorcycle accident. Her lower leg was severed. Stacy collared her so she wouldn't see her leg was gone and talked with her in the ambulance all the way to the hospital. Five years later, Stacy was subpoenaed to testify for Alex, the plaintiff in her own personal injury case. The injured young woman's last name was different, but Stacy remembered every detail of that night, down to what the twenty-one-year-old girl was wearing when she had to cut her clothes off to check for further injuries. Alex won her case due, in large part, to Stacy's testimony. That experience taught her how important it was to note details at the scene of an accident.

When Stacy retired from LAFD after twenty-four years of service in 2015, her wife, Petra, was there. One of the most meaningful notes came from SFFD Chief Joanne Hayes-White, who sent Stacy a congratulatory note and her own personal challenge coin. A challenge coin is a tradition derived from the military; firefighters and police officers stamp challenge coins for their department and always carry them with them. If not, the legend has it, they must buy a round of drinks for the bar. Even LAFD Chief Ralph Terrazas also gave Stacy his own personal challenge coin. Los Angeles Mayor Eric Garcetti issued a proclamation, invoking Stacy's nickname in the fire department, Sister of the Revolution. Her advice to any young girl interested in becoming a firefighter is, "Just be proud of who you are. You are probably going to come up against some negative commentary, but the infrastructure in the upper command of LAFD has so many more women now. You have an engaged fire chief and mayor so harassment isn't going to be tolerated. There's a very strong women's organization to support and mentor you. There will be bumps in the road but it's just a great job."

Petra's goal in the fire service is to have fun. She joined the fire service to be outside, ride on a big red truck, bring calm to chaos and, ultimately, to make a difference in people's lives. Besides Stacy, Petra's had great mentors: Dany (Danielle) Cotton, the poster girl for the London Fire Brigade, now Fire Commissioner of the London Fire Brigade. She is the first woman to be awarded the Queen's Fire Service Medal in 2004, and in 2007, she became the highest-ranking woman in the British Fire Service with the post of Area Commander. There's also Adele Phemister, who did twenty-five years and promoted just one rank, a tiny lady, marathon runner. "I'm still friends with her. These two were at the open day where I tried on all the gear, performed some tests and they said, 'You'd make a good firefighter.' When I left that day, I had a huge grin on my face because I'd found my calling. I would add Katherine Ridenhour, retired Battalion Chief, Aurora Fire Department, Colorado. I met her at my first women's conference. She was a party girl, loved dancing. I loved dancing, so we shared a friendship," said Petra.

Most calls to fire departments these days are medical emergency or car accident calls. In LA, 85 percent of 911 calls are medical emergency calls. That's why paramedic training is key. In England, Petra may not have pulled someone from a burning building, but she's rescued four kids from trees, no injuries. "We do more rescues than fires," she said. She would advise young lesbian firefighters, "Just go for it. It's the best job in the world. It beats working for a living."

"Just be proud of who you are. You are probably going to come up against some negative commentary, but the infrastructure in the upper command of LAFD has so many more women now. You have an engaged fire chief and mayor so harassment isn't going to be tolerated. There's a very strong women's organization to support and mentor you."

Stacy Taylor

With a dash of Dutch courage, she bought a placeholder titanium ring, brought a vial of glitter, sang, "Christmas bride," got down on bended knee and asked Stacy to marry her in a horse-drawn carriage in Vienna just as it started to snow.

Petra Barneveld

Katerina Blinova: Refugee to Award-Winning Computer Scientist

Software Engineer
Dolby Laboratories, Jan. 2007 - Present
UC Berkeley 1998 Outstanding Achievement in
Computer Science Award
Uzbekistan Refugee

Growing up in Uzbekistan, Central Asia, Katerina Blinova and her mother lived behind a metal door to their apartment in a high-crime area. Blinova was a Jew living in a predominantly Muslim country. On her way to school, she and her friends were verbally harassed and attacked with stones thrown by gaggles of young boys. Katerina and her mother were not physically safe and, economically, without a future. When under Russian control, Uzbeks were considered second-class citizens, so when the Soviet Union broke apart, the country wanted to elevate the dominant majority of Uzbeks. The situation in Uzbekistan became untenable for Russian-speaking people in general and Jews in particular.

In 1991, after the break-up of the Soviet Union, Blinova's mother, Olga Grinberg, applied for refugee status as part of a family reunification program the US had set up for Jews from the former Soviet Union. After two years and lots of paperwork and what seemed like an interminable waiting period, Blinova's mother and Katerina were granted visas and refugee status after their long-awaited interview at the American Consulate in Moscow.

Katerina came to the US when she was eighteen, knowing practically no English and little about the culture she was about to be immersed in. Jewish Family Services proved a lifesaver to the family, introducing Katerina and her mother to key contacts and helping them set up life in the US. Fortunately, Katerina's aunt preceded them and lent social support during the transition. For the first six to nine months, Katerina barely understood a word of English. She had studied Russian and German in school. It took years to learn

English well enough to express her personality. The hardest part of coming to the US was the language barrier.

Katerina Blinova and her mother, Olga, did not come to the US with a huge bank account. In fact, they required government aid and food stamps as refugees. Katerina

Katerina Blinova and partner, Emily Coles,
at Tour Eiffel

actually got a job in 1994, a little over a year after coming to the US, as a software configuration manager for TRW Financial Systems in Oakland, CA. This was again due to the kindness of strangers. One of Katerina's professors at Laney College worked with the company's internship program and encouraged Katerina to apply. She won the internship and, then, was offered a job. She stayed with that company thirteen years and it suited her. The job worked around her school schedule and allowed her maximum flexibility.

It was a contact met through a San Francisco volunteer who took Katerina around to San Francisco Bay Area colleges and universities. Without that, she would never have gone on to University of California at Berkeley in the field of Computer Science. Back in Uzbekistan, Blinova studied applied mathematics at a technical college, Tashkent State University. UC-Berkeley awarded Katerina Blinova its 1998 Outstanding Achievement in Computer Science Award for her amazing academic achievement, graduating from the top computer science school in the country with a 3.98 GPA, never scoring lower than an A- in all her CS courses.

Though Katerina's done well in this culture, she feels she is a hybrid. "It's hard to explain. Half my heritage is Jewish, half is Russian. But I don't practice Judaism. I've now lived in America for more than half my life at this point. So I'm more American than anything," she said.

Even though Katerina may be curious about Uzbekistan, it would be hard to go back. Everyone she knew growing up has left. More of her college classmates from the Soviet Union are here now. She could go to the physical places where she grew up, but all those places have changed. When people who left go back, there's the threat of extortion or worse. People realize that you left for the US, so going back there would present many risks. "There's nothing to go back to; everything's different," Katerina said.

When asked if she was a lesbian in Russia, Katerina replied that she didn't even know what that was when she was growing up in Uzbekistan, then part of the Soviet Union. It was only in her thirties that Katerina realized she was a lesbian. "My mother was sad. She didn't cry or anything. Periodically, she would tell me about male prospects, even after I told her I was a lesbian. She would have liked me to marry a man and have children and all that. But she met all my girlfriends and she liked them. 'I don't want you to be alone, so if that's what it takes, then alright,'" she explained. So, with grudging acceptance, her mother learned to adapt to her only daughter being a lesbian. Her father, Russian, stayed behind in Uzbekistan and accepted Katerina's declaration with no questions. This was just before he died in 2015.

Katerina found community in the world of ballroom dance. She began taking community classes at Lake Merritt Dance Center in Oakland with lesbian dance teachers and competitors Zoe Balfour and Citabria Phillips. Her first international competition was at the Gay Games in Cologne, Germany, in 2010. She was amazed by the hundreds of couples, and that was just women dancing with women.

Lucky enough to land white collar jobs, Katerina met many Americans who welcomed her as a newcomer. Off a job board, she landed a software engineering position

with the foremost sound engineering company in the
world, Dolby Laboratories. She just posted her resumé, was
called in for an interview by Dolby's internal recruiter,
interviewed by several managers, and called back that
same evening with a job offer. Katerina took the job and
has been working at Dolby ten years now. Being gay was
never an issue. Being a woman engineer was never an
issue. With "exceeds expectations" performance reviews,
raises and stock options, Blinova has thrived in the Dolby
environment. She likes it there because she can grow
and learn within the company, changing groups and
departments and fields of study easily. She's worked with
the cinema theater management group, the cinema sound
processor group, and the content creation group.

For her, there have been no barriers to entry to the field of
software engineering. But she admits she may be the wrong
person to ask because one of the positive things about the
Soviet Union was that there was real gender equality.
Women could work in any field. It never even occurred to
Katerina that she couldn't do what she wanted to do. So, she
studied what she loved—math, science and computers. To
her, barriers never crossed her mind.

She does realize, however, that her experience is somewhat
unique. Women in the US are not encouraged to enter
STEM fields. The former Harvard president Larry Summers,
in fact, suggests that one reason there are relatively few
women in top positions in science may be "issues of intrinsic
aptitude." And while he acknowledges that discrimination
exists, he generally plays it down as a factor. His attitude
and remarks are not uncommon in STEM programs at

universities throughout the US. So while she sees in her own efforts to hire qualified women that there is a problem with supply, Katerina's never been in a situation where anyone at Dolby rejected a female engineer who was a strong candidate for the job.

Katerina Blinova as a child in Uzbekistan.

Photo taken by her father

Still, Dolby Laboratories began company-wide conversations about diversity in 2016. The hiring process is being examined. This has never happened before. Katerina is the only woman engineer in her group and she's unaware of any demographic data published by her company. It is only since Salesforce.com began publishing demographic data of its employees that other high tech companies have begun to follow suit. Google, for example, acknowledged that only 19 percent of its technical workforce was women in 2016 (Google Diversity Report, 2016).

Her advice to young queer immigrants or refugees would be: "Work hard. Be yourself. When I came here I benefited from a few very important people in my life. Social resources are very important. Try to find community. Like-minded individuals. People who want to do the same things as you. People who live in this country are fairly friendly and want to help. Find them and ask for their help."

Katerina wants to help new immigrants herself by paying it forward. She benefited from Jewish Family Services and the English Center for International Women at Mills College in Oakland. She's looking for ways to give back to those new immigrants and refugees coming to the US for the first time.

She would also say to queer refugees who may have come from countries like hers where to be queer is forbidden, illegal or risky, "Be safe, first and foremost. You don't have to be an activist. You can enjoy the freedoms other people have fought for before you. Obviously, find community. Find other people you can feel comfortable with—queer people and queer people from your home country."

Katerina has found her place in America. At age forty-two, she has now lived here more than in Uzbekistan. She's in a long-term relationship with American dance teacher Emily Coles. They've been together six years, and three years ago, they bought a house together in San Francisco's gay neighborhood, the Castro. On hearing that Scorpio, her birth sign, is the sign of transformation, of the Phoenix rising from the ashes, Katerina agreed. "It's happened "but I only want to do that once."

"Work hard. Be yourself. When I came here I benefited from a few very important people in my life. Social resources are very important. Try to find community. Like-minded individuals. People who want to do the same things as you. People who live in this country are fairly friendly and want to help. Find them and ask for their help."

Katerina Blinova

Jose Comoda and Chris Phan: Asia Pacific Dancers Stun Judges at the 2010 Gay Games in Cologne

Jose Comoda and Chris Phan, First Southeast Asian World Champion Latin Dancers

They had never danced before in an international competition. The European judges had never seen nor heard of them. When the "A" Finals were over, a slim Vietnamese and petite Filipino dancer won Silver in the Men's Latin Ballroom Dance Competition and Gold in the Senior I - 35+ category. Among Czechoslovakian, German and American tall and imposing dancers, it's surprising that the equally tall European judges with the handmade German shoes even saw them.

Chris Phan came to the US when he was sixteen, ten years after his parents submitted a request to leave Vietnam and waited in Vietnam for those papers to go through. He did not begin ballroom dancing until he was twenty-six and graduated from college with a civil engineering degree. While he "wussed out" of becoming a dance teacher as he had wanted to do, he was able to return to ballroom dancing in his free time once he had a "good job."

Coming out was not a problem for Chris. When he was twenty-six, his father took him aside and said, "Chris, I know you're gay and that's okay. Just be safe." It would be ten years before he told his mother, who thought he was experimenting, until she saw him perform in a same-sex dance number at the Cowell Theater in San Francisco. It turned out that her boss was in the audience that night and when Chris saw his mother, he saw the look of shock on her face. When his mom got to work on Monday, her boss couldn't stop talking about the performance and Chris—she loved it! After that, things went pretty smoothly and his mom comes to any local competitions.

Jose Comoda came to the US from the Philippines when he was nineteen. The death of his father when he was seventeen pushed Jose, a pre-med student, into secretary school so he could help his mother and family. It would have been alright to come out in the Philippines, but Jose would have been expected to be flamboyant and to dress as a woman. Here, in the SF Bay Area, he could be gay in any way he chose, and "that was very liberating."

Once he was making his own money, he began to take modern jazz dance classes. His teacher told him he was talented but needed a foundation to improve his lines. Ballet was that foundation and led to his winning a scholarship to the SF Ballet School. Until age twenty-six, Jose was a professional ballet dancer, dancing for small companies and choreographer showcases throughout the SF Bay Area. After his retirement from ballet, Jose joined the Robert Moses' Kin Dance Company and traveled and performed modern dance all over California. That "gave me my performance sense. Robert, a straight man, picked me up and danced lead with me—I was his leading lady; now, that took courage at that time." When Jose left ballet and professional dance, after having injured nearly every joint in his body, he learned Pilates as a way to rehab and return to dance quickly. Studying with some of the world's most prominent Pilates instructors, Jose became a Pilates instructor, a fitness trainer, and a classical ballet dance instructor. A visit to his doctor turned up a surprisingly high cholesterol flag on a blood panel and Jose was advised to do more cardiovascular exercise. "I hated it. I had a flyer for same-sex ballroom dance with a photo of Zoe Balfour and Citabria Phillips on my refrigerator for a year before I decided to try it," he said.

It was always all about the dance for Jose, but when he began partner ballroom dancing he was accused of "looking too much like a ballet dancer." In fact, when Zoe suggested he dance ballroom with Chris Phan, his private coaches said in the first session, "You'll never make it." By European standards and even American dance standards, Chris Phan and Jose Comoda had started too late and did not have the profile of classical ballroom dancers. International ballroom dancing—Standard and Latin—are the last bastions of heterosexual hegemony. A man leads and a woman follows. Neither two men nor two women are allowed to dance with one another in straight competitions. Same-sex ballroom dancing "breaks barriers. We become ambassadors for our sport and our LGBTQ community," Jose enthused. In fact, Jose and Chris both have danced in the straight ballroom world with straight women, playing the traditional roles of lead and follow. But the Gay Games are nothing like the straight ballroom dance world. Dancers from all over the world mingle regardless of level or country.

So when Jose and Chris won their first competition in April of 2009, Jose cried. "Jose is more emotional than me. I asked him, 'Why do you cry whenever we win?' and Jose said he cried to honor his overcoming all those objections to becoming a competitive ballroom dancer."

Are they ever afraid? Always. Jose wants to "puke" every time he gets on the floor to compete. Chris got so nervous at the Gay Games in Cologne that he almost missed his quarterfinal heat by hiding in his hotel room and telling Jose to ignore the incessantly ringing telephone. "Don't answer it. I'm too stressed." But, thankfully, Jose answered the phone to his first teacher Zoe Balfour's Welsh accent and breathy voice: "Boys, the quarterfinal heat is on and you must come down to the ballroom now." They raced into the Maritim Hotel ballroom on the Rhine River just in time for their round.

Besides defying convention and dancing in public as two men, the most daunting challenge for Jose and Chris dancing International Latin—which includes Rumba, Samba, Cha-Cha-Chá, Paso Doble and Jive—was that they were "too nice" according to their Lithuanian world champion dance coaches, Vaidas Skemelis and his wife, Jurga Pupelyte. So Vaidas would make the competitors do sliding doors, and each time they turned, they had to say, "F--- You!" until they embodied the character of the dance. In an exercise for the Cha-Cha, they were encouraged to do the "dirty Cha-Cha." This took the same-sex dancers from good with musicality and technique to great with emotion and togetherness. In fact, when they won in Cologne, the judges' comments were, "You were the most together. You had the greatest connection," one of the highest aims in ballroom dancing. Rather than the typical male Latin competitors, posing to the audience or the mirrors individually, Jose and Chris embodied same-sex partner dancing.

Jose and Chris never strove to win. They strived to improve from competition to competition. In fact, often, Chris didn't want to compete. "I never feel ready and if I'm not ready, I don't want to do a sloppy job. Jose is a professional dancer. He knows *the show must go on*," he said.

It would have been
alright to come out
in the Philippines,
but Jose would have
been expected to be
flamboyant and to dress
as a woman. Here, in the
San Francisco Bay Area,
he could be gay in any
way he chose and "that
was very liberating."

Jose Comoda

When he was twenty-
six, his father took him
aside and said, "Chris, I
know you're gay and
that's okay. Just be safe."

Chris Phan

Today, at age forty-nine, Jose
Comoda holds onto his connection
with the gay community as a
seven-year veteran of the same-
sex ballroom formation team,
headed by Greek Cypriot dance
teacher, Photis Pishiaris, Vima
Vice Squad. Vima is the Greek
word for step. Chris Phan, now
forty-two, joined the Vima Vice
Squad for the 2016 April Follies,
the longest-running, same-sex
North American Ballroom Dance
Competition. Vima Vice Squad
has taken Gold in North American
competitions seven years running.
Jose comments, "It's always been
fun. It's not about the *self*. You
don't outperform everybody. You
do everything with everybody. I
get to dance with my boyfriend
who's not an experienced dancer.
He feels he's not up to par. He's
wanted to quit so many times.
Talk about courage. That takes
courage. Dancing with him is
such a joy." At this, Jose teared up.
"Dancing is not about winning or
showing off. It comes from the soul.
Dancing lets me tap deeper into
my soul. It's not what I want to
do; it's what I have to do."

· 244 ·

Though Chris was torn because he always wanted to be a dancer and his Asian parents wanted him to be a doctor, a lawyer or an engineer, "I'm pretty happy with my life. I always make the best of things. I'm pretty happy-go-lucky. I let things roll off." This was evident in Cologne the last night of the Gay Games when we all took public buses to the Closing Ceremonies and several skinheads began harassing Chris and Jose on the crowded bus, calling them disparaging names in German, which some of the group understood. Chris just smiled and ignored them, diffusing what could have been a very volatile situation. Brave. That's real-world brave.

Jacqueline Grandchamps, PhD: Vive la France!

Founder, French Escapade
Belgian-US Citizen
Former Cancer Researcher, Stanford University
Married to French Co-Founder of French Escapade, Valerie Sans,
Fulbright Scholar

On November 3, 2016, the fifteen-year wait to be together was over. Jacqueline (Jac) Grandchamps, PhD, Founder of French Escapade and Belgian-US citizen, and Valerie Sans, Fulbright Scholar in the US and French-born citizen and English teacher in France, are able to live together at long last. France legalized same-sex marriage in May of 2013 and the US did the same on June 26, 2015, making it both practical and possible for the two to live together.

Jac Grandchamps founded her unique travel experience business in order to be with the love of her life. French Escapade promises, "Don't Be a Tourist. Be Our Guest." The first trip we took with Jac to the Rhône Valley and the French Alps, Jac's partner, Valerie Sans—from the tiny village of La Côte St. André—cooked gourmet French meals for a small group of six while Jac took us in a mini-van on daily adventures: to a Medieval city, to a fifth generation chocolatier, to a village market, to a stone-driven walnut oil maker, to the French Alps, and to an eleventh-century Carthusian cloistered monastery with signs posted, *Zone de Silence.* As promised, every evening in the Chelieu farmhouse was akin to living in a French village as the French live. Some mornings, we even walked the cobblestone paths to the bakery in town for warm, fresh-baked croissants and French bread.

In business since 2003, Grandchamps has led more than 150 trips with more than 1,500 guests. Honestly, the business was created so that Grandchamps and Sans could be together. They were never apart more than six weeks. Valerie would come to the US during her summer and winter breaks. In winter, Jac was not working the travel business, so they would have six weeks together. "I don't think we would have done it if we only saw each other once a year."

The best part of the business is "meeting the people. They are in a group of friends, usually. They are on vacation. They are in a good mood. There are lots of stories and laughter,"

Jac Grandchamps and Valerie Sans, married in Valerie's village; Co-Founders of private tour business French Escapades

Photo by Martina Datz

said Grandchamps. What does she like least? "Dealing with people's problems. Some people don't share my beliefs; it is not a problem for me. As their guide, I cannot start arguing with them. Some people don't like other people in the group, but I have to make sure everyone's included."

Even when Jac and Valerie are in the US, they share a European lifestyle. "The food. People in the US eat anytime. In Europe, it's at specific times and people don't eat snacks. In the US, Americans snack all day. For us, the food is the most important. And, at home, we speak in French to each other. We don't speak English together. We watch the French news, no TV commercials during the thirty-minute news. In the US, there are commercials every three minutes."

When Jac and Valerie married in 2015 in Valerie's village of 5,000, home to Berlioz, the composer, the right-wing Mayor of La Côte St. André married them. It was the first gay wedding in the village. The Mayor said it was the biggest wedding in the town's history. Valerie's neighbors, in their 70s, asked to come to the ceremony. They wanted to witness history. Friends and family walked the cobblestone streets tossing rose petals at the happy couple. Everyone was happy, except for Valerie's mother, who refused to attend, citing social propriety. Valerie's mother did not accept it. She calls Jac Valerie's friend. The laws may be liberal, but social acceptance lags far behind. Jac's mother attended, but "only because no one knows me there," as Grandchamps' mother is from Belgium. For Jac's mom, it is the same as for Valerie's mom: she does not want Jac to tell her mom's friends or refer to Valerie as her wife. For the married couple, it was one of the happiest days of their lives. "Even if it seems like a long time coming, we never thought same-sex marriage would be legal in our lifetime. I think it's great. In a way, it was quick. Actually, when we got married, we thought it would not make any difference other than paperwork and getting to live in the US together, which is a big thing. But we

Grand Chartreuse Monastery Founded by St. Bruno in 1084, founder of Carthusian Monks. Located in the Chartreuse Mountains, north of Grenoble, France Jac Grandchamps, Tour Guide

Photo by Kathleen Archambeau

didn't think it would make a difference in the relationship. But now, formally calling one another wife, not partner, not friend, in a way, we feel a bit stronger with each other. Official for us. Official for others."

The road to this point has not been smooth. Grandchamps came to the US as a post-doctoral fellow doing cancer research at Stanford University. After getting her PhD at University of Liege in Belgium and completing her three-year post-doctoral studies in molecular biology, she found she did not like working alone in a research lab. So, she changed careers to IT, becoming an expert in customer interface and usability for World Savings and other start-ups. For her third career, motivated by love, she began a travel business.

The work aspect of the changes in Jac's life turned out to be the easy part. In 2010, Valerie Sans was diagnosed with Stage 3 ovarian cancer. After a year of traditional Western medicine treatments which involved surgeries and chemotherapy, Sans took her health in her own hands and went to Germany to seek alternative medical treatment that taught her how to eat healthier, following the strict Budwig diet—no sugar, no flour, no dairy, no meat, daily doses of flaxseed oil—and how to reduce her stress through visualization, meditation, and breathing exercises and cognitive therapy techniques for changing her perspective. The French healthcare system only paid for traditional treatments. That is when Jac turned to the LGBTQ community to raise the money for Valerie's life-saving alternative medical treatment. They reached their goal in a month. As a thank you, Grandchamps hosted a dance party at a run-down alternative church space in downtown

Oakland. Valerie, her hair grown back, was radiant. And Jac was beaming. In January 2011, Sans was pronounced by doctors cancer-free. In 2016, she remained cancer-free, passing that critical five-plus year mark. "After five years, it doesn't mean you never get it back, but it is a milestone," she said.

Fortunately, France offers its lifetime-appointed teachers generous time off to recover. After a year of paid leave, Sans returned to the technical school in her village working in the library part-time. Now that she is married and has a spouse who works in the US, Sans is allowed to take a one-year sabbatical, up to ten years, to be with her spouse. At the end of ten years, Sans will be sixty-one, and after twenty-seven years of teaching, will be able to retire with nearly full healthcare and retirement benefits.

Valerie has always loved the US, so she was excited to live there full-time with her wife. If she could never go back to her flat in her tiny village, she would not have been so happy. But, with Grandchamps' thriving business—now eight painting tours in France, Italy and Spain, two cultural tours in France and Spain, and two cooking tours in France and Spain—Valerie will be able to go back to Europe for months at a time. "I will never be rich running this business, but it is enough for me," she said.

Has Brexit adversely affected Jac's business? "Very few people from England are coming to my trips and we have no trips to England. So, Brexit doesn't affect me. The Great Recession in the US and Europe was tough as it was much harder to secure travelers at that time. But, now, business is booming. And, many painting teachers have heard of my trips and want to do a trip with me. They bring the students. So, it is not so hard for me."

If you are a LGBTQ Belgian or French young person, I would advise, "Do not be ashamed of yourself. It may not be easy. Especially when you are teenagers. Some boys, especially, can be mean. Still you have to be true to yourselves. Be who you are—especially now that the laws are positive in Belgium, France, and the US. As far as starting a business, being gay or not being gay, there is no difference."

As for bi-national couples, Jac advises, "Make adjustments to make it work. If you only see each other once a year, it would not work. Today, there is Skype. That made a huge difference to us. No large phone bills anymore. If Valerie bought something—you know how she buys at least one new scarf or purse a year like most French women -- she could show me. So, Skype really helped us."

"Even if it seems like a long time coming, we never thought same-sex marriage would be legal in our lifetime... But now, formally calling one another wife, not partner, not friend, in a way, we feel a bit stronger with each other. Official for us. Official for others."

Jacqueline Grandchamps, PhD

Jim McSweeney: Curating a Safe Space

Manager, Gay's the Word
Highlighted in the 2014 feature film *Pride*

Only Remaining Gay Book Shop in the UK
Manager Since 1997
Gay's the Word, 66 Marchmont St., London, WC1N1AB

Gay's the Word is the last remaining lesbian and gay bookshop of three in the UK and the only bookshop featured in a film about the National Union of Mineworkers (NUM) strike from 1984-1985. Two seemingly dissonant events converged when Lesbians and Gays Support the Miners (LGSM) organized from the action center of the gay bookstore on Marchmont Street in Bloomsbury, London. They collected money for the miners outside the shop every Saturday. In the longest strike in England's history, 26 million work days were lost. When the LGBT community first offered to help miners in Wales, some miners rebuffed the help coming from "pouffers and dykes." However, as the strike wore on, the LGSM group hosted a popular "pits and perverts" concert and raised money for the families of miners suffering without jobs or support from other unions in the country.

In a heartwarming story of the unfolding of the unlikely alliance, the 2014 feature film *Pride* tells the little known story of Mark Ashton, leader of the London chapter of LGSM, collecting money outside the Gay's the Word bookstore. Roger Ebert called the film, starring Bill Nighy, Paddy Considine, and Imelda Staunton a film designed to "make its audience stand up and cheer. Here, a true story that could have been played as straight drama, yet the filmmakers opted for a lighter approach to capture hearts and minds. The Brits do this type of crowd-pleaser far better than Hollywood."

The last scene of the film, the London Gay Pride Parade in 1985, could have starred Jim McSweeney, Gay's the Word Bookshop staffer since 1989, and parade marcher as early as 1984. Jim is not the typical activist. In his own words, he is a gentleman. This has served him well for the twenty-seven years he has managed the bookshop that is part community center, part activist meeting place and most decidedly, a repository of literary and historical LGBT fiction, nonfiction, and poetry.

In the window of the small and narrow shop, opened as the first gay bookshop in England in 1979 on Marchmont Street, are black and white photos from the film, *Pride*. People from all over the world come searching for the shop featured in the film. Pink triangles figure prominently on the bookshop sign. A gay flag adorns the window, laden with books and everyday names like Alan Hollinghurst, Sarah Waters, and Emma Donoghue. Man Booker Prize-winner Anne Enright's novel, *The Green Road*, is highlighted as a gay character anchors the novel by one of Ireland's most celebrated authors. Notices of readings and book signings appear in the window.

When the shop was threatened with closure due to rent increases in 2007, the LGBT community stepped in and contributed to keeping the doors open. Sir Ian McKellen sponsored a shelf. Many gave in £100-increments to keep this treasure alive.

A quotation from Sarah Waters trails above the cash register. In a September 30, 2011 review in *The Guardian*, Waters reveled, "It was with tremendous excitement that I discovered Gay's the Word bookshop in the early 1990s. In those days, it was rare to find lesbian and gay books in mainstream shops and libraries, so seeing shelf upon unembarrassed shelf of queer books and magazines was an exhilarating experience "Simply stepping through the door felt like an act of self-affirmation "It is mainly, however, a thriving contemporary bookshop and it always repays a visit."

A group of lesbians have been meeting for free in the back of the bookshop for thirty years. At a time when there were few gathering spaces outside of bars for women, Gay's the Word offered a safe space to commune and talk. A transgender group meets once a month. A Gay Black Group was started by one of the bookshop workers. Over the years, many LGBT groups have used the free space at Gay's the Word to network and support one another. All are welcome. "That's the great pleasure of working here, is the variety of people who come in, people from all over the world, people of different ages, talking about books, but sometimes talking about film or theater. I hear people's stories. It is a privilege. I do feel like I am curating the space and holding it and, of course, selling books, but more than that. Engaging with the community that feels like extended family," McSweeney said.

Jim comes from a large Irish Catholic family from Cork, Ireland. He has a twin sister who campaigned, along with her husband, for the gay marriage referendum which passed by a two-thirds majority vote in May 2015. Jim was home for the celebration. "My sister even appeared in one of the commercials as an extra. It was really full on and very moving to see. Seeing the city I left, with banners and posters in pubs, straight pubs like the one across the street from my house. There was a wonderful feeling when the results came through when I went to the campaign center and talked to the activists there. And I felt very proud of being Irish as well, that it was finally about full acceptance and not having to hide," he said. This was a very different Cork than the Irish city McSweeney left back in 1982. Ireland, one of the most Catholic countries in the world, was also the first in the world to pass gay marriage by popular vote.

Storefront of Gay's the Word Bookshop on 66 Marchmont Street in Bloomsbury, London
Timeout, London

When Jim came to the UK, he was twenty-two. He hadn't even been sexual until he was twenty-one. "What I loved about the gay marriage campaign in Ireland was the emphasis on family and family members. Mothers, fathers, sisters and brothers all showed up and talked about equality for the family. To remove what we do sexually in the same way that I couldn't care less what straight people do in bed and to show us as people and that the cause is about love and respect and what we contribute to society was brilliant," Jim said.

 The Catholic Church, the Church of England, and the Catholic cardinal in Scotland launched vicious attacks on gays at the same time young priests accused that same Scottish cardinal of sexual harassment during the same-sex marriage referendum debate in England. They lost the battle, and same-sex marriage was legalized in England in 2013 and came into force in 2014.

At this point in mid-life, Jim is single and relaxed about it. At one point, he was doing the scene, but these days he's more interested in seeing his friends, going to films and to the theater. Not surprising, since Jim first came to London to pursue a career in acting. Friendship is very important to him. Jim feels that gay people are especially good at friendship. Many LGBTQ people of Jim's era had to create a network of strong friendships because family and society might have rejected them. They might still. This, perhaps, explains the furtive way a young Polish gay man asked Jim about gay magazines, or the quiet titter from a young Korean girl reading from the lesbian fiction bookshelf the day in 2016 that I interviewed Jim McSweeney.

Ireland, which Jim "loves completely," was twenty years behind the UK when he left in 1982. Ireland was a monoculture at that time. Jim had never met anyone with divorced parents or knew anyone who lived together before marriage. Even more strikingly, Jim never met anyone openly gay in Cork, Ireland, when he was growing up. Jim was deeply in denial about being gay during his teens. While living in London, he discovered there had been a gay club in Cork for years before, so he made sure he visited it when he came home to visit family.

Making a living in London, in what amounts to a nonprofit bookshop—governed by a board of contributors who never made a dime back from their investments and who re-invest any profits back into the bookshop—is more challenging than ever. Rents in London are sky-high, on par with San Francisco and New York City. Fortunately, Jim lives in a council flat, one of many built in the '30s, '40s and '50s for ordinary working people all over London. So, his rent is "normal, not market rate."

Though the bookshop is doing well and has seen a resurgence of interest in the gay bookstore since the film came out in 2014, Jim's always worried about the next rent increase. Though owned by Camden Council, because of so many government cuts, the Council has to make as much money as possible with its properties. The last rent increase was 30 percent, which the shop negotiated down to 25 percent. But, fifteen years ago, a rent increase was more like 10 percent, which you might negotiate down to 8 percent.

"Celebrate who you are and when people say it's wrong or against God's way of being or that it's abnormal, just dismiss that and know it's nonsense. You get to redefine your masculinity or femininity and so just celebrate who you are. And the quicker you learn to accept yourself; you can get on with your life."

Jim McSweeney

New generations are discovering the LGBT bookshop. In a report of the American Booksellers Association, the number of independent booksellers is up 27 percent since 2009, and book sales are up 7.5 percent in 2015 from 2014.

Bookshop lovers and avid readers find Jim McSweeney a delight. His literary sensibilities guide his book choices and they appear to be unfailing. His twenty-seven years of running a gay bookshop is testimony to his service to the ever-changing and, sometimes, fickle tastes of the queer community.

His advice to young queer people is equally sagacious: "Celebrate who you are and when people say it's wrong or against God's way of being or that it's abnormal, just dismiss that and know it's nonsense. You get to redefine your masculinity or femininity and so just celebrate who you are. And the quicker you learn to accept yourself; you can get on with your life. If I'm thinking about when I was young and very intense, it's just important to remember that this, too, will pass. I would just say, too, that a sense of humor goes a long way."

Peggy Moore: A Woman of Faith

Senior Special Advisor, Mayor of Oakland, 2014-2016
Campaign Manager, Successful Oakland
Mayoral Race for Libby Schaaf
Captain, 551 California Delegates, DNC 2016
Presidential Campaign
Statewide Political Director for Organizing for America,
DNC project
California Political Director, President Obama's
2012 Re-Election Campaign
Founder of Sistahs Steppin' Out in Pride, 2001-2011
Former President East Bay Stonewall Democratic Club
Political Consultant

Growing up in an Oklahoma public housing project, Peggy
Moore never dreamed she'd meet the President of the United
States. Never imagined she'd host Barack Obama during
his four-year re-election campaign as the California Political
Director for the 2012 re-election campaign. Never imagined
she'd manage a successful mayor's race for a major American
urban city.

Peggy's mother was director of the choir at her Pentecostal
home church. Every Wednesday and Saturday night, the
family lived in church for rehearsals and went there for all-
day services on Sundays. When Peggy Moore first realized
she was a lesbian, nothing in her upbringing was positive
for that path. The Pentecostal church saw believers as those
who could "speak in tongues," not use those tongues for any
other purpose. Her mother's religion called Peggy's sexual
orientation a sin. She prayed God would heal Peggy.

And, in a way, God did. When Peggy Moore was in junior
college, she had this moment when she realized that it was
not religion but her relationship with God that was most
important. "I just got still and celebrated that relationship.
Once I let go of all that stuff I was taught in church, I was
able to get past those many years of not knowing how to
blend being a lesbian and a woman of faith."

That faith deepened when Moore came to Oakland in
1990 and met Reverend Eloise Oliver of the East Bay
Church of Religious Science. Pastor Oliver helped Peggy and
encouraged her to see herself as a reflection of God.

Peggy Moore adopted her new home of Oakland, CA and made it her own. Her email says it all: moore4oakland. She's served as President of the East Bay Stonewall Democratic Club. She, along with a core group of community organizers, founded Sistahs Steppin' Out in Pride, an outreach effort to embrace lesbian women of color in Oakland. What began as a march around Lake Merritt of about one hundred women of color evolved into an inter-generational lesbian community event that attracted thousands over its ten-year period of engagement.

With a background in outdoor advertising with ClearChannel Outdoor, Moore was the point person with community and nonprofit organizations. Her work on the Barack Obama election campaign led her to become Deputy Field Director for Northern California and into the arms of Hope Wood, a Latina-Anglo LA Clippers Girl and community organizer.

Moore and Wood's story is a classic. It was love at first sight. They kissed on October 7th and moved in together before Thanksgiving. "Crazy! I've never done a U-Haul before. That's the first time I've done a U-Haul," the fifty-two-year-old Moore exclaimed. Moore's African-American friends were wary of the fair "woman of color" Peggy was dating. But, as Peggy tells it, "Hope was all in. I wanted someone who was diggin' on me like I was diggin' on her. I needed somebody who understood that I was going to be engaged politically, but also somebody who had their own spiritual practice so we could celebrate and share that together. It's definitely a grounding spot for us." Moore and Wood have been together since the first Obama campaign and married for three years.

Following the successful grassroots Obama campaign in California, Moore became the statewide political director for the Democratic National Convention Organizing for America project. Her offices were in downtown Oakland, but she traveled up and down the state facilitating and engaging the next generation of voters. During Obama's 2012 re-election campaign, it was Peggy Moore who was responsible for accompanying Barack and Michelle on every visit to California. That meant, many times, opening for the President at gala and private fundraising events.

After Obama's successful re-election in 2012, Moore was tapped by former Governor Jerry Brown's (then Oakland Mayor) former Executive Assistant and Oakland City Council Member Libby Schaaf to run her city-wide campaign for Mayor of Oakland. In a crowded field of fifteen candidates, Moore's task was daunting. How do you portray a straight, white, upper-middle class lawyer representing the wealthier hills of Oakland as a champion for the entire city of Oakland? Moore helped craft a campaign for one of the only Oakland-born candidates, "Made in Oakland," that became a successful rallying cry across the divide of African-Americans, Asians, Latinos, and others that make up one of the most diverse cities in the US. Moore had "street cred" with the African-American community and helped Libby bridge that gap. Moore took a lot of flak for not supporting the African-American candidate, nor supporting the lesbian candidate. As in all things Moore undertakes, she wanted to support the best

candidate for the job. Her integrity would not allow her
to do otherwise. Libby Schaaf won in decisive fashion in
2014, and Moore was one of her first appointments as Senior
Special Advisor to the Mayor.

*Peggy Moore, Campaign Manager for Libby Schaaf's
successful Mayor of Oakland race and community
organizer/wife, Hope Wood*

In Peggy's role as Senior Special Advisor, she started a program called Restorative Justice Circles, which facilitates small group discussions between the Mayor and underrepresented minority youth from the Oakland Unified School District. So far, one hundred youth have met personally with the Mayor to voice their concerns. Since 2014, Moore has worked with community partners to employ more than 3,300 youth in the Summer Jobs program. Beyond jobs, Moore trains employers on how to bring in the youth and coach and mentor them not only on job skills, but on life skills. "I recognize the adult piece of the training is just as important as the youth piece of the training," she said.

Moore is a bridge builder. A collaborator. Despite the bruising world of politics, Moore remains positive and upbeat. "I don't take stuff personally. There are layers and layers of pain and if I wanted to make that my story, I could. But, there's also so much good, so I'm always trying to err on the side of good," she explained.

Maybe that's why Peggy Moore was chosen as the Captain of the 551 California Delegates to the 2016 Democratic National Convention. Her job as "whip" was to unify the 330 Hillary delegates with the 221 Bernie folks and ensure that all voted. At one point, the Sanders camp was demanding to see the Clinton's camp credentials. Moore put a stop to that. In fact, when the votes were read by Governor Jerry Brown of California, Moore was crouched down below the podium, literally keeping the Sanders' folks from grabbing the mike and disrupting the proceedings.

An innate ability to "meet people where they are, at their core" has brought Peggy Moore from the projects to the President's suite. That ability to listen, to engage across differences and to disagree respectfully, has led Moore to affect change all up and down the State of California, back home in Oakland and all the way to the White House. In 2016, Moore decided to take up the mantle of representing all of Oakland by running for the only at-large City Council seat. Endorsed by the Mayor of Oakland, Moore championed affordable housing, transit-oriented sustainable development, responsive government, restorative justice, and state and federal investment in Oakland. She lost the contest, but won many followers with her approach to governance.

Moore's mother is still Pentecostal, but she's never backed off her love of her daughter. She embraces Peggy and Hope into the extended family circle, the whole clan gathering in Alabama for a family reunion this summer. She's still burdened by the church teachings. Just recently, "my niece came out. My mother was shocked and saddened. I'd been out all these years. I was thinking to myself, really? I had to recognize she still has stuff around it."

Peggy Moore does not take on "other people's stuff," even her own mother's.

Her approach to people is, "You don't know nothin' about nobody. There are so many stories that make up who a person is, triggers you'll never know. I try not to have a lot of judgment."

When asked about her identity, Peggy replied, "African-American. As soon as I walk into the room, there's nothing I can do about that. I mean that's just everywhere I go." What advice would Peggy Moore give to young African-American queer youth? "Trust your instincts. Be yourself. Find kindred spirits. Don't ever doubt the value of who you are." Peggy Moore has learned to embrace her own innate gifts and use them for the greater good.

"Once I let go of all that stuff I was taught in church, I was able to get past those many years of not knowing how to blend being a lesbian and a woman of faith."

Peggy Moore

Andreas Ozzuna: *Don't Cry for Me, Argentina*

Originally from Buenos Aires, Argentina
Small Business Owner
Married to Business Partner, Citabria Ozzuna
Wooden Table Baking Co.

For many years, Andreas Ozzuna did what was expected of her. She went to school. She got a good job as a geologist at a water treatment plant. She worked eight hours a day. She followed her mom's example. She admired her father and his family, all entrepreneurs, but he left Andreas when she was nine, so that dream went out the door with him.

Then, one day, the water plant didn't renew her contract. "I was kinda' thankful that this freed me from my 'duty' to do something, I didn't know what it was gonna' be; I had no plan except that I wanted to bake and cook and make things," she said. So, at age forty, Andreas Ozzuna became a small business owner, leasing a kitchen and launching Wooden Table Baking Co. in 2011.

The bakery really started with Andreas' *abuela*. As a small girl, Andreas and her grandmother cooked together, rolling out raviolis, empanadas, and *alfajores,* Argentina's national *dulce de leche* cookie. "First, my business was called Buenos Aires Alfajores and I had to change it because that was the advice that I got. If I was going to build a brand, if I was going to make other products, I had to expand the name. And that was a big thing for me because I was attached to that name. After thinking about it a lot, it turned into Wooden Table Baking Co. I had to *feel* the name. When it was Wooden Table Baking Co., that was my grandma's table, it made total sense to me. It brings back that memory. I loved my grandma. So I wanted her to be a part of it."

Andreas grew up in her grandmother and grandfather's house in Buenos Aires. "We have lots of cousins. Family in Argentina is not only your sister, it's your cousins and your cousins' cousins. So, I grew up in a large extended family. All the family members would show up at our house. My grandma cooked for everybody."

Andreas' grandmother died two years ago; Andreas didn't know how much her grandmother knew about her business. She had some sort of Alzheimer's. She wasn't able to talk. But maybe some part of her brain understood because whenever Andreas visited, her grandma smiled.

Ozzuna started her business going door-to-door. She sold her alfajores to local cafes, specialty stores, and high-end markets. How she got into Whole Foods Markets was kind of a fluke. An Argentinian friend was in a local market and tasted a competitor's alfajores. He told the bakery manager that he had a friend whose cookies were better. The manager asked Andreas to bring in some samples. Then, the manager of the local store contacted the regional office in Emeryville. "When the door opened, I knew if I didn't walk through, I might regret my decision. I wasn't expecting a lot because I am a small ant in the world. But the Whole Foods Regional Office in Emeryville, CA did call and wanted me to bring my alfajores. I went and brought the cookies. The guy said, we like them, but can you make them a little smaller? And that's how it started. I said sure."

It was difficult at first, going from a handful of small mom-and-pop markets to thirty-six grocery markets. Andreas didn't have a way to melt that much chocolate. So she and her wife, Citabria Ozzuna, launched a Kickstarter campaign to raise money for a chocolate enrober and cooling tunnel. Before, they were making the chocolate alfajores one by one.

So, they had to gear up for thirty-six Whole Foods stores, thirty boxes a week. The queer community, her adopted family in the US, came through, raising $33,000 in less than six weeks.

The most frequent Argentinian visitor to the States is Andreas' seventy-two-year-old mother. Last Valentine's Day, her mom came after taking a chocolates class. "Let's make chocolate," she said. Andreas said, "That's cool. When you come over, we'll do something together. And that's how the whole thing started. She started making *bon bons* with *dulce de leche* for the business. We do alfajores with chocolate so I know the timing and crankiness of it. The chocolate can easily go wrong. You need patience and attention to detail. I made them and they weren't so great in the beginning." Andreas practiced and practiced. There was a lot of trial and error and learning from her mistakes. She worked with the candies to extend their shelf life. The first batch is going to stores this week.

In 2015, Ozzuna reached another milestone. She went from leasing a small kitchen several days a week to owning her own kitchen, operating five days a week. She launched the new kitchen with a Tango performance and Open House in time for the winter holidays. Now, Wooden Table Baking Co. employs eight people, six in production and two in the front office, including Citabria Ozzuna, Andrea's wife, the Director of Marketing. The company bakes more than 4,000 alfajores a day. Does Andreas still enjoy what she does? "Oh, yes, I still enjoy alfajores. The cookie is awesome. The espresso chocolate. When I make espresso alfajores, I try not to eat too many. I have a few. I try not to bring them home. I'll eat them. I still like the traditional ones, too."

Does Andreas feel she's made it now that she's been in business five years? "Uhm, I made it in a way. Depending on what *made it* means. If it means, do I make a lot of

Andreas and Citabria Ozzuna on their wedding day.

Photo by Luis Costadone

money? No. We keep going. We're a very young business. It has a long way to go. I feel that I've made it in a way, personally. I'm doing what I'm supposed to be doing and I enjoy it. It makes me feel free. In that way, yes."

Andreas (middle, front row) and crew, Wooden Table Baking Co., Oakland, CA.

Photo by Luis Costadone

The LGBTQ community supported Andreas Ozzuna in so many ways. "Now I'm married and have a family in the US. If it wasn't for all the people who believed in me, encouraged me, really supported me in many, many ways, probably I wouldn't be here," she said.

Now the alfajores line includes everyday favorites: traditional, gluten-free traditional, chocolate, chocolate mint, Chipotle chocolate, and lemon ginger. Seasonally, chocolate peppermint and pumpkin spice are customer favorites. In 2016, Wooden Table Baking Co.'s dulce de leche bon bons hit the Northern California market.

Ozzuna wants her employees to be happy to come to work. She has people who've been with her since the beginning. She holds meetings every other week, listens, and asks: how can we make things better and easier? The production staff speak Spanish, as does Andreas. That makes communications flow easily. She prevents Repetitive Strain Injury (RSI) by rotating people. No one does the same thing every day. One day, the chocolate room. One day, the dough. One day, the packaging. Everyone is cross-trained. This way, the staff can empathize with each other and never have to do the same thing every day.

The Queer Tango community has also supported Andreas in growing her business. When they have events, they announce her cookies. She contributes to raffles and donations. She brings **alfajores** to *Milongas*. She sometimes sells or donates to the USA Tango competitions and events.

Having wife Citabria Ozzuna on-board as Director of Marketing has been very rewarding. For a long time, Andreas wanted her wife to work in the company because she likes to have family involved. American Citabria was always around the company, but got more into it this last year. "I was extremely happy. I see her at home and at work, too. It's kind of fun. I like it. But, sometimes, it's hard to stop talking about the business. It's eight o'clock at night, we have to say: let's cut it and talk about other things," Andreas said.

When Andreas arrived in the States, people gave her a job because she was a lesbian. That was really cool for her. "In Argentina, if you're a queer person, a lesbian, you don't get the job because of that. No matter how smart. If you're a lesbian, you don't get the job. Here I got the job because I was a lesbian."

Her vision is to keep doing what she's doing, to develop new products. Eventually, she wants to open a storefront, against everyone's advice. She still has the urge to do it. "If you never try, you never know. I don't want to die without trying," she said.

The scariest moment in owning Wooden Table Baking Co. came in preparing for an audit for the first time. One has a great responsibility with food safety and the public. It's a third-party audit, and most major distributors and retail grocery stores require one. The baking company scored 915/1000. Not only did they pass, that score was the equivalent of an A.

"I'm very lucky to be doing what I'm doing. The least I can do is give my best. Bringing Argentina, integrating the food and Tango culture into the American entrepreneurial culture, is really, really cool. People like the products and embrace the alfajores and bon bons and the culture baked into them," Andreas explained.

Her best advice: "Be yourself. Be the best you can be. And as one queer immigrant from South America to another: *You can do it!*"

"Now I'm married and have a family in the US. If it wasn't for all the people who believed in me, encouraged me, really supported me in many, many ways, probably I wouldn't be here... In Argentina, if you're a queer person, a lesbian, you don't get the job because of that. No matter how smart. If you're a lesbian, you don't get the job."

Andreas Ozzuna

Eric and Mat Rosswood: Journey to Same-Sex Parenthood

Eric Rosswood, Author, Husband and Stay-At-Home Dad
Mat Rosswood, CFO, Littler Mendelson-Mendelson P.C.,
Husband and Dad

Gay dads are a fairly new concept. Especially for those gay men who have become fathers independent of heterosexual relationships. So when Eric Rosswood, author of *My Uncle's Wedding,* a children's book for ages four to eight, and *Journey to Same-Sex Parenthood,* one of the first nonfiction books to tackle the subject from the point of view of LGBTQ parents, became a gay dad, he never dreamed he'd be living in Kansas, married to Mat Rosswood, with their openly adopted three-year-old son, Connor.

As a queer activist, Eric had been doing AIDS Walks, volunteering with LGBT centers, and agitating as a youth advocate for as long as he could remember. "I started a Gay-Straight Alliance at my high school when I was seventeen. I was OUT at school, between sophomore and junior years in high school in San Diego. It was received well by some people and badly by other people," he said. Eric endured anonymous bullying. For example, someone spray painted on a wall, "Eric sucks dicks." Students sprayed one of the ceiling tiles purple and started writing Eric's name and the names of his friends on it. There were groups of kids who would suck on hard candies and throw them at Eric's friends so the candy would stick to their hair. His mom was afraid that something worse was going to happen to Eric, so she tried to stop him from being an activist. Eric aggressively created change and acceptance. His mother tried to reel him in from being so out there—not just out, but active. At the time, Eric thought his mom was not accepting. Looking back, Eric sees it as being more protective. Eric's older brother is a drag queen, so his parents had experience with a gay kid already. His parents have been very supportive.

Eric Ross met Mat Wood in 2007. They got married on April 2, 2011 and combined their last names to Rosswood. They just hit their five-year anniversary.

How did they meet? Eric was working fourteen hours a day, seven days a week for months. He had just moved up to the San Francisco Bay Area. He didn't want to meet people at the bars. He wanted to meet people for activities, for social activities, not necessarily to date. So he was looking online for hiking groups, coffee clubs, for groups where he could do everyday activities. He saw someone looking for a same-sex dance partner for Salsa. It's not something he normally would have done, but he thought, "Nobody knows me up here." He decided to do something completely out of his comfort zone. If he was horrible and embarrassed himself, at least no one he knew would know, so he just went for it.

He met Mat and they hit it off, really hit it off, becoming partners on and off the dance floor. "It's funny because I actually knew within minutes of meeting him that 'he was the one.' That's odd because that's never happened to me before. And I know people talk about love at first sight, I honestly knew within five minutes. We met first for lunch and I was already quizzing him on things," Eric said.

Yes, Eric's always wanted children, "but I didn't think it was going to happen. I didn't know how to make it happen. And I thought at times it would be something I would have to give up, sadly. Our community has evolved a lot over the years. Society told us that being LGBTQ is wrong, and so many people had dual identities with secret relationships. A lot of people didn't invite friends or lovers over to their house because they didn't want their neighbors to know that they were gay. They didn't want people at work or they didn't want their roommates to know that they were gay either. Lots of people in our community resorted to going to bathhouses to meet people in private or they'd sneak out alone to the gay area to go to a club where they could have a sense of belonging." Anti-LGBT beliefs from society made queers live lives in secret, but living in secret only fueled the belief that what queers were doing was wrong. Why else would it be done in secret, living in the shadows?

It was a vicious cycle that was hard to break, but over time, in the last couple of decades, it's shifted. Queers are more accepted: it's okay if neighbors know; it's okay if friends come over. Shortly after adopting Connor in an open adoption Eric and Mat planned for years, Mat's company moved from San Francisco to Kansas City, Missouri. Eric and Mat moved to Overland Park, Kansas and were able to build a house—something extraordinary in California, but easier in Kansas, a state with a much lower cost of living. They moved from one of the bluest states to one of the reddest states. "I was very nervous. Kansas is a very conservative state. I was worried because we had a kid. I was worried about how accepting the schools would be. How accepting neighbors, society, restaurants would be. We've been here over a year so far and everyone's been accepting. It's been great," Eric said.

Eric and Mat interviewed a lot of schools. Some of them were not quite there yet, not 100 percent accepting. But other ones had gone through the thought process of how to be open to everyone. They changed enrollment forms to say parent and parent, not mother and father. Not all of them, but some of them. Some schools had books on diversity, including same-sex parents. Some did not. Kansas is very Republican; however, Overland Park seems to be in a liberal pocket because everyone has been so accepting.

It's definitely a possibility that Eric and Mat and Connor are the first gay family some people have seen in Kansas. They've made a point to meet other LGBT parents. Last week, they went to a Modern Family Alliance group and had a picnic.

There are LGBT families everywhere. One of the states with the highest percentage of LGBT families is Mississippi. That state was one of the last holdouts against gay adoption and just lifted the ban. So, sometimes the states that are most against it can actually have the highest population.

When Eric and Mat were contemplating adoption, they couldn't find what they were looking for, and someone told Eric if you can't find it, just create it yourself. Eric wanted the perspective of people who had been through the experience, hearing other stories from other LGBT parents. So Eric began to write *Journey to Same-Sex Parenthood*. Eric did a lot of research—two years—beforehand. He's a Libra, so he constantly evaluates the pros and cons of everything. Open adoption for his family was just right. Eric and Mat liked the idea of being in contact with the birth mother.

There are so many challenges with open adoption:

- The birth mother can back out after you and your partner/spouse get emotionally invested

- The birth mother can change her mind any time before the birth

- The waiting pool takes a long time

- There are often many false starts and, sometimes, scams which are emotionally challenging and stressful

- The entire process is out of your control

- There are legal risks

- Ensuring parental rights are secured is paramount

Both Eric and Mat are on the birth certificate as Connor's legal parents. Birth certificates—beyond heritage and genealogy—serve a greater purpose: enrolling the child in school, proof you have the right to make medical decisions, and legal rights/protections from the outset. This is especially important when leaving the country as Eric and Mat and Connor do to visit Mat's parents and sister in England, where Mat's from originally.

Open adoption can cost $30,000 to $40,000. Surrogacy can cost more than $100,000 (extracting, fertilizing, storing eggs, hormones, birth). So both routes create a financial burden. Prospective parents need to plan for and take this into consideration. International adoption poses further risks, both legal and financial with inter-country laws. Open adoption is fairly new—just 30 years—and more common in the US than anywhere else.

The Family Equality Council, Our Family Coalition, and Gays with Kids, are just some of the groups Eric reached out to when conducting research for his book, asking what went well and tips and advice. It was a very long process of collecting data. Eric's book, *Journey to Same Sex Parenthood*, was the culmination of stories told in their own words by LGBTQ parents who took the uncommon journey to parenthood. Mat wrote their story. March 2016 was the publication date. Eric promotes the book online and via conferences, including LGBTQ conferences, family equality conferences, and via his webinar on LGBT parenting. Eric is active on social media—Facebook, Twitter, and Instagram. Eric plans to write more books now that he's a stay-at-home dad and Connor is in preschool two days a week.

Now settled in Kansas, "Connor already has a best friend which is awesome. They're in soccer together. And we've hit it off with Connor's best friend's parents. And we did just meet up with the Modern Family Alliance, so Connor is able to see other families like ours."

Eric's advice to LGBT couples contemplating having children is: "There are so many different ways to go about it. One of the most important things to have is patience with yourself and your partner during the research phase, patience during the waiting period. Don't listen to whatever anyone tells you. Not even me. Get as much information from all perspectives.

Go with the flow. Be sure to keep some date nights. Make that a priority—couple time is so important. You need time alone to nourish your relationship with your partner/spouse because the state of your relationship trickles down throughout the household."

Mat Rosswood

Kansas is as misunderstood by those who've never been there as San Francisco is misunderstood by those who've never been there. It's seen as a very, very conservative place. It's friendly and diverse. There is a group here called the Modern Family Alliance out of Kansas City. It's family-oriented.

"While it's interesting to have same-sex parents in our social network so that we have perspectives for Connor that show him he's not the only person who has two dads, parents generally have an awful lot in common, without respect to their sexual orientation. We just had breakfast with an opposite sex couple who have a child in preschool with Connor and the discussions we have about, you know, what's it like to have a three-year-old, are the same. It actually creates a bond between parents because it isn't gender-based," Mat said.

After adopting Connor, Eric and Mat's lives became much more family-oriented than before. They gravitate to friends who also have children. While still very close to all the friends they've made over the years, those who don't have children want to go out or go away for the weekend and they can't do that because they have Connor, and that changes the dynamics.

Mat first thought about being a dad when he was in college. His perspective at that time was fostering a gay teenager and helping them go through the experiences that he had experienced as a teen with more of a guide than he had at that point in his life. "It wasn't until I met Eric that I started to think about having a baby. And if you'd asked me five years ago, would I have become a parent in the way I've become a parent, then I would have said no. Not!" he said.

Whereas twenty to thirty years ago, most people married in their twenties and had two children before their thirties, there's a lot more diversity in that family structure today. Mat's company, Littler Mendelson, where he is the Chief Financial Officer, has supported his being out as a gay man and a gay dad. "They've been awesome. Littler Mendelson is a labor law firm built upon diversity. I've reached a point in my career where being authentic in the workplace is really important to me. It's the reason I explored the firm before I joined the firm. The Chair of our Board is a lesbian; members of the Executive Team are LGBTQ. We filed an *Amicus Brief* in the Marriage Equality Case before the Supreme Court. My personal experience was identical to any other parent in the firm," he said.

It's funny how life works. Mat looks back on his sense of a family unit from how he grew up—his father was the breadwinner and his mum stayed home when he and his sister were small kids. He finds himself emulating his parents, though it wasn't the life he had imagined as a gay twenty-year-old. Even marriage brings a different set of responsibilities. "Having a baby just makes you drive a little slower. Think a little more consciously about what you say. It's kind of like one of those life experiences that makes you stand back and say—who am I? Am I the person I want to be, not just for me, but now for my husband and my son? What example am I setting? It's a great way to grow and be part of the design of how we grow," he explained.

Mat's from England and went to university in Bath. England has moved ahead in the many diverse ways there can be to achieve parenthood. When Mat lived in England, he never seriously contemplated being a father. He left the UK twelve years ago and knows more about American gay adoption than English gay adoption.

"We haven't experienced any gay dad phobia in Kansas so far. We experience the same challenges as any parents: are we doing the right thing for our son?" he said.

Mat is Pop and Eric is Dad. Both their parents were excited about being grandparents again. Watching his parents, or Eric's parents, interact with Connor, "you would never know Connor was not our biological child by the way they interact." They see Eric's parents who live in San Diego more, and Mat's parents from England, at least twice a year. Technology fills the gaps with FaceTime on a weekly basis.

Connor, too, enjoys FaceTime with his birth mom. Legally, both his birth parents have rescinded all parental rights. The law around that is pretty water-tight. One of the beauties of open adoption is that Connor's birth parents are part of his life. "Connor's birth parents have found some level of peace with the decision that they have made since they see how happy Connor is and how well-loved and cared for by his gay dads in Kansas," Mat said. Unlike a closed adoption, where there are the lingering, ongoing questions—*Did I do the right thing? Where is my child?*—Connor's birth parents not only know where Connor is, but have contact with him.

"We're considering having other children. Three, I'm told. I come from a family of two children; I have a younger sister. Eric has four brothers, he's number four. They've all met Connor. One brother has two boys; one brother's boy has a boy. Lots of boys on that side of the family. As uncles and cousins, they're fully embracing of Connor," Mat said.

Kansas public schools rank in the Top 10 in the country. One of the surprises in Kansas was the quality of the public schools. Eric and Mat both went to public school— having a real social experience was part of the experience. They want Connor to learn about life as much as he learns about academics.

Mat's advice to prospective LGBTQ Parents: "I don't know how you decide whether you're ready or not. It's a very personal decision. I don't think you should be fearful. It's a phenomenal experience. I put that alongside meeting Eric. It's an amazing journey. It's a real gift. It's not a toy; it's something you have to be really ready for. When we first started the journey, I found myself incredibly angry at all the hoops we had to jump through, relative to a biological parent. I now believe because I didn't enjoy the ease of being a parent, biologically, as an openly gay man, I'm a better

"I don't know how you decide whether you're ready or not. It's a very personal decision. I don't think you should be fearful. It's a phenomenal experience. I put that alongside meeting Eric. It's an amazing journey. It's a real gift. It's not a toy; it's something you have to be really ready for."

Mat Rosswood

"Don't listen to whatever anyone tells you. Not even me. Get as much information from all perspectives Go with the flow. Be sure to keep some date nights. Make that a priority—couple time is so important. You need time alone to nourish your relationship with your partner/ spouse because the state of your relationship trickles down throughout the household."

Eric Rosswood

parent as a result. I had to really think about what it meant to be a parent before I became one. Choose the path best for you. Build support networks and go for it. Of course, I also recommend getting a copy of *Journey to Same Sex Parenthood* by my husband and gay dad, Eric Rosswood. It's filled with tons of tips and advice from same-sex parents to help other prospective parents in the LGBT community navigate the path to starting their own families."

Gloria Soliz, MDiv.:
Never a Drag

Founder of The Last Drag, LGBTQ Smoking
Cessation Program, 1991-present
Co-Founder, Coalition of Lavender Americans on
Smoking & Health (CLASH)
Co-Chair of the Covenant Council, Bethany United
Methodist Church (UMC), San Francisco
Member, The Reconciling Ministries Network of the UMC

"My ambitions are not to have money, have a big house or to have a big car "it's really to help people and to make a difference not only in people's lives, but in our society."

Gloria Soliz has been making a difference in the queer community since 1991, when she established The Last Drag, a smoking cessation program tailored for the LGBT community. She's not a smoker, but she does care passionately about public health. Smoking is the number one cause of preventable death in the United States and around the world. Lesbians are three times as likely and gay men twice as likely to smoke as the general population of California. Of those eighteen-to twenty-five-year-old smokers, LGB smokers make up 45 percent of that group. Anecdotal evidence suggests that the Transgender community smokes at an even higher rate for obvious reasons; however, official studies are limited.

Back in 1983, when Gloria Soliz got her Master of Divinity degree from the highly respected Pacific School of Religion (PSR), affiliated with Berkeley's Graduate Theological Union, the Church wasn't prepared to have a Hispanic working-class lesbian who didn't speak Spanish be appointed a United Methodist Church (UMC) pastor. Gloria Soliz didn't fit the stereotype. She couldn't be categorized in a box the powers that be could check off. During the ordination process, people didn't really get a glimpse of Gloria's ability to think more deeply, to hold on to thoughts and to pursue ideas like *Grace* in the interview. Soliz used to read Kierkegaard and Tillich for fun. But her interests in feminist and liberation theology weren't of any interest to the Board of Ordained Ministry. "It was really hard for me to stay closeted. My

spirituality and my coming out came at the same time.
I didn't experience them as a conflict for me, but it was
a conflict for the church. The more I came out, the more
punitive language showed up in the *Book of Discipline* of
the UMC. It was disappointing that people did not recognize
my call to the ministry, of course. On the other hand, I am so
grateful for my education. It's the one thing that has pulled
me out of poverty, not just economically, but, academically,
intellectually, and socially," she said.

Why would a trained minister get involved with queer
smoking cessation programs and policies? "I think I was
almost homeless at the time. I really needed a job. And I had
to decide if I wanted to come out or not. You remember the
time. I was asking myself, 'if I take this job in this lesbian
community clinic, am I ever' to get another job again?' I was
just looking at it as a job, and it ended up being a career, a
mission and a ministry."

Gloria has worked continuously in the smoking cessation
field her entire career and trained traditional health
providers from the California Department of Public
Health, the American Lung Association, the American
Heart Association, the American Cancer Society, Kaiser
Permanente, and UCSF Medical School on how to reach
out to the queer community who suffer smoking addiction
disproportionately. Smoking, it's been found, is more
addictive than heroin or cocaine. So, learning to quit
smoking, in the context of a gay community often relegated
to bars for social life, especially in the early days, became
a question of health equity. Soliz is hypervigilant when it
comes to any hint of injustice or inequity.

Soliz has testified before California's Tobacco Education and Research Oversight Committee and influenced smoking cessation policies in California. California has declared smoking a health hazard and prohibits the smoking of tobacco in public indoor spaces, restaurants, bars, workplaces, and vehicles receiving state funds. Violators are subjected to escalating fines. In 2016, Governor Jerry Brown signed into law raising the minimum smoking age from eighteen to twenty-one. These laws, coupled with a tobacco tax dedicating monies to smoking cessation programs and anti-smoking advertising targeting the ill health effects and the degradation of one's "looks," have reduced smoking in California to the second-lowest rate in the US, 12.9 percent, compared to the state with the lowest rate, heavily Mormon Utah, at 9.7 percent. Soliz is most proud of her role in shaping policy in California.

When facilitating The Last Drag groups, when clients are trying to quit smoking, oftentimes they'll say, "I'll just smoke more marijuana," as if that would solve the problem. Just like the general public, the LGBTQ community has gone through a process around recovery programs. People in recovery would never say that they're going to replace one addiction for another. But the people who have not really looked at their lives or their lifestyles will turn to alcohol, other drugs, and marijuana. "It's a really unfortunate thing. When my Last Drag clients first try to stop smoking, I don't want to discourage them. So, I oftentimes let them say they'll just smoke marijuana. Then, we go on to other things. Later on, when they've tried to quit and they're not successful, I have to bring it up, right? If they look at all things together, marijuana, other drugs or alcohol addiction, they may get into recovery and, then, are more likely to be successful quitting smoking as well because they finally see it as an addiction. In recovery, you have to get honest and real pretty fast," Soliz explained.

Despite not being ordained, Soliz did not turn her back on the United Methodist Church. She's serves as Co-Chair of

Gloria Soliz, facilitator, The Last Drag Smoking Cessation Program for the LGBT community

the Covenant Council of Bethany UMC in Noe Valley, San Francisco. Often the only Mexican-American Methodist in the room, she's constantly reminding her fellow parishioners of the call to: *Do all the good you can. By all the means you can. In all the ways you can* "As long as ever you can, attributed to UMC founder, John Wesley. Soliz has served in myriad ways. She's played with Bell Appeal and sung songs accompanying herself on guitar for the Children's Service. Responsible for the altar, she's created "art installations," like the pride balloon rainbow arch over the altar for the Pride Sunday Service in June. She's served on nearly all the committees in her thirty-six years involved with Bethany's Community of Faith. A lifelong Methodist, Soliz has no intention of walking away from a global church that serves the underserved and is often the first to respond to disasters around the world. UMC has many resources, and Soliz wants to tap into those resources for the greater good. "We don't always like everyone, but we love them. We're all a little quirky, including me. It's hard to take the Methodist out of me. Funny, isn't it? It's more challenging to be OUT as a Christian, a member of Bethany United Methodist Church, than to be OUT as queer in San Francisco. But, I believe in my heart that there are more positive things going on in people's lives than not," she said.

Today, Gloria Soliz probably would have been ordained as a UMC minister because the Board of Ordained Ministry, particularly the Western Jurisdiction, has sidestepped the *Book of Discipline* by not considering sexual orientation, but, rather, the candidate's gifts and graces as the main criteria for ordination.

Inside or outside the church, Soliz connects with the LGBTQ community. Bethany often prides itself that roughly 50 percent of its members are from the LGBTQ community. Gloria is also a member of The Reconciling Ministries Network of the United Methodist Church, a coalition of Methodist local churches that are welcoming and affirming of LGBTQ members, pledging to "transform the church and world into the full expression of Christ's inclusive love." "I'm committed to keeping the UMC as open and liberal as possible," Soliz said.

Soliz has been consistent in serving the queer community, with over twenty-six years of serving the community through The Last Drag and CLASH, thirty-six years with Bethany United Methodist Church, and twenty-eight years with The Reconciling Ministries Network. Her commitment level is high, like everything Gloria Soliz does. For this, Soliz has been recognized with numerous awards, including:

- Outstanding Community Service Award, Alameda Co. Tobacco Control Coalition, 2011

- Local Hero Award, LGBT Pride Month, KQED, 2010

- Award of Excellence, CA Department of Health Services, 1992

- Achievement Award, National Gay and Lesbian Medical Association, 1997

As for advice she'd give: "First of all, I wouldn't give LGBTQ youth advice. I'd ask questions. Ask for their opinions. Share the research. Start a conversation. Unfortunately, one of the things that happens when we are *told not to do something* is that we tend to rebel. Our subconscious doesn't recognize NO and only hears, SMOKE." And that's the last thing The Last Drag pioneer Gloria Soliz wants queers to do.

"First of all, I wouldn't give LGBTQ youth advice. I'd ask questions. Ask for their opinions. Share the research. Start a conversation. Unfortunately, one of the things that happens when we are *told not to do something* is that we tend to rebel. Our subconscious doesn't recognize NO and only hears, SMOKE."

Gloria Soliz

Christina Yin: Shanghai to Sacramento

Senior Programmer Analyst
CA Dept. of Healthcare Services, Sacramento, CA
Member of the China Moon Dance Troupe

Christina Yin grew up in two worlds. She spent half her childhood with her grandmother in Shanghai and the other half of her primary school years with her parents in the little village of Xinfan in the Chengdu Province of China. Her parents survived the Great Chinese Famine of 1959-1961, a made-up crisis called a natural disaster by the Chinese government as China tried to pay back loans to Russia in food, starving their own people. Yin's parents worked in a manufacturing factory, making coded copper wire for all electronics devices and lived in the agriculture-rich village where the government moved the factory and 600 workers from Shanghai. Yin's parents were good Chinese citizens. They were proud to help the government shield its military-related products from intruders near the coasts, so they gladly volunteered to leave Shanghai. They obeyed the one-child rule and had only Christina and, because of government benefits for those complying with the one-child rule, were able to give Christina a richer life than her classmates.

As a child in Xinfan, many children came to school without shoes. They were always stealing Christina's pencils. So, one year, her mother bought pencils for all the children. Some kids were so hungry that they died of hunger. When Christina came to the school, she was five and younger than the other children who started school at age seven, so her classmates called her a "princess from Shanghai." She was bullied by students and teachers alike.

When her mother tired of the responsibility of a headstrong Christina, she shipped her off to her own mother in Shanghai. The bullying started all over again, with sophisticated

Shanghai students making fun of the "country bumpkin with the funny Mandarin accent."

Not until about fifth grade did Christina learn strategies for winning over her classmates. "I had good genes, so I began to grow," she said, and she learned to dance with visiting dance teachers from Chengdu, the capital of Sichuan, who taught dance in Christina's village. Christina was a natural. She was both flexible and tough. Other kids would whine or wouldn't try the moves. Christina not only was able to perfectly imitate her teachers, but she could express the meaning of dance. She was asked often to demonstrate for the other kids. She had a good understanding of music. This made her sought after by her classmates for annual productions and variety shows on special holidays, like Chinese New Year's and May Day.

Soon, Christina was choreographing dances for annual talent shows. "I realized that not everybody thinks like me. Most have a hard time remembering the sequence of the dance. For me it comes to me intrinsically," she said.

Every night at her grandma's house, her grandmother told her a story before she went to sleep. Christina became quite the storyteller. So, her Xinfan classmates soon realized that she had stories to tell them about the "big city" of Shanghai, and the Shanghai students realized she had stories to tell them about the interior countryside of Xinfan. As an extrovert, Christina used this gift to her advantage and soon was included wherever she lived.

Christina was asked to become a professional dancer and study at the Chengdu City Music and Dance Troupe. At first, studies were fun. But once it became serious, Christina didn't enjoy it much. There were strict rules about height and weight. As everyone in China knows, to become a professional athlete, musician or dancer, one must give

Christina Yin (R) with her wife, Mexican immigrant Ruby Nieto

up everything else and devote 90 percent of the time to training and training and training. It's very competitive. A Chinese professional dancer may dance for two to three years and, then, when younger dancers come along, the professional is out. Teachers, once encouraging, became very "picky" and were always comparing students. The fun had gone out of dance for Christina and, fortunately, her parents did not want her to have such a narrow life, so they didn't push her to continue to study as a professional dancer.

Christina loved computers and business and studied both at a three-year technical institute in Zhangzhou. After working for an Australian medical devices company, Yin felt she had a pretty good grasp of English. She went to an American university based in Shanghai. While at Armstrong University in Shanghai, Christina took business courses in English. She completed her BA while working as a liaison for American professors in China at the university. It was there she met her "American mom" Mary Anne Brady.

Dr. Brady lives in Oakland, CA, and Christina kept in touch with her via email even after Mary Anne left China. They had grown close when Christina was helping Mary Anne navigate everything from trains to menus in China. In fact, Mary Anne used to fax Christina a restaurant menu and Christina would circle the dishes she knew her professor liked. So, it was no wonder when Christina came to the US on a six-month business visa that Mary Anne invited her to stay with her for a month while she got settled.

Soon after, Christina moved in with roommates near Cal State University East Bay, hoping to pursue an MBA. She soon found out that her credits didn't count and that she would have to repeat half her courses because they had been taken in Shanghai, not in America, even though she'd taken the courses from an American university.

That is how Christina Yin came to study jewelry. She secured a K-1 vocational visa by going to the California Institute of Jewelry Making in Carmichael. The seven-month course cost $13,000 up front. Christina had saved $14,000 and paid the tuition all at once for the school. She worked as a waitress and bartender while going to school and became a bench jeweler for the next four years. Her English dramatically improved.

She found camaraderie in the China Moon Dance Troupe, an amateur group of engineers who loved to do Chinese folk dance in Sacramento. That was in 2002. Christina landed a job with the California Department of Health Care Services as a Senior Programmer Analyst Specialist, heading up the web services team. That was nearly ten years ago, and Christina still loves her job. She's working with Medi-Cal and Medicaid, burgeoning programs, so she's never bored. Her dance troupe is made up of fellow technical professionals as well as dancers, so the esprit de corps makes Christina feel at home away from home. The group is so good that they were asked to perform the halftime show at the professional Sacramento Kings basketball game on January 18, 2017. They're regulars at the California State Fair and Chinese New Year's celebrations in and around Sacramento, California.

The biggest surprise of all came when Christina realized she was a lesbian. It wasn't until her thirties and it wasn't until she was in the United States. When she was in high school in China, she thought she wanted to be a boy. Then, she could protect her girlfriends, make them happy, write them notes, and bring them flowers. She snuck into the library and

Christina Yin, center, China Moon Dance Troupe,
Sacramento, CA

read about the operation and didn't want to do that, but was very confused because she didn't have the same sexual feelings for boys that her girlfriends had and she got jealous when her girlfriends found boyfriends and spent less and less time with her. She even thought maybe she'd marry a boy, have a child, then divorce him and raise the child alone. In China, being a lesbian was still considered a mental illness and Christina didn't want to be "cuckoo."

When Christina Yin came to the United States, she began watching movies and reading books about lesbians. She went to a random dance event at a church and found other lesbians interested in same-sex ballroom dancing. She started to "hang out" with this group of gays and lesbians and found herself having a lot of fun. She watched the movie, *Saving Face,* and realized that she was like the main character with the disapproving parents. This explained so many of the contradictions she felt growing up in China.

In 2007, Christina came out. She wanted to come out to everyone. Her parents had since retired and returned to Shanghai. Their co-workers from the factory were also their friends. The most important thing to Christina's mother, who was so proud of her daughter and her accomplishments, was "saving face." When Christina landed a job in the United States, Christina's mother bragged to all her colleagues. When Christina sent her parents pictures and videos of the China Moon Dance Troupe, her mother bragged about her daughter. To her mother, Christina was the smartest, prettiest, best girl in the world. Until she came home and showed her parents the movie, *Saving Face,* which she had a friend get a Chinese version of for them to see. Midway through the movie, the main character and another girl kissed. Christina's mother stood up and made Christina stop the movie. "What kind of American movie are you making me see? I never heard or saw such a thing," she had said. During the many discussions that followed, all Christina's mother could admonish was, "Why do you have to tell me? You live in the United States. Who cares what you do there? Why don't you bring a handsome man back here and I can throw you a big wedding. You get all the presents. Then, you go back to the United States and do whatever you like. You don't have to talk about it!" Christina's mom told her not to tell anybody. Don't tell the relatives. Don't tell the friends. Her mom was mad the whole trip. She couldn't brag about Christina in front of her friends anymore.

That was in 2007. The same year she came out to her parents, she came out to the dance troupe which proved to be a non-event. At the end of 2007, Christina fell in love with a veterinarian and fellow same-sex ballroom dancer. She wanted to talk about it. She wanted to bring her girlfriend home to her parents and did so in 2009. Of course, her parents told everyone that Christina's girlfriend was her "friend." Christina's mom didn't want anybody to know the true story.

But Christina had already told many of her peers in China, the younger generation and they, in turn, told their parents, the older generation. Even her mother loved one of the biggest talk show host stars in China, Jin Xing, a former male ballet dancer and Army colonel. The male-to-female openly transgender talk show host draws 100 million viewers a week. She's very popular in China and Christina's mother loves her and all things Hollywood. So, with the Internet, books, movies, and major Chinese television shows, China, too, has become more open. As has Christina's mother.

After Christina split up with her first girlfriend, she met a Mexican immigrant at a professional meetup in Sacramento. Ruby Nieto came to the US when she was seventeen, but didn't come out until her thirties. The two were like pepper and salt: Christina, the extrovert and Ruby, the introvert. Together they forged a deep bond. They hiked and cooked and gardened and danced together. Soon, they made the commitment to marry. Christina wanted her parents to give her away.

Remarkably, in 2012, Christina married Ruby Nieto in a wedding attended by both her parents. Of course, it was easier to honor their only daughter's wedding nearly 7,000 miles from home. Still, they came and were happy for their

"Be brave. Ignore those who do not accept you. You know better. Forgive them. They haven't had a chance to learn or be exposed to anyone different. Most people will come around to love you for who you are eventually."

Christina Yin

daughter that she found someone to love and spend the rest of her life with in the US.

Her advice to any young Chinese lesbian would be, "Be true to yourself. You have to know and love yourself before anyone else can love you. Don't be afraid. Be true to your true self. You're still who you are. Be yourself. Forget the label. Be brave. Ignore those who do not accept you. You know better. Forgive them. They haven't had a chance to learn or be exposed to anyone different. Most people will come around to love you for who you are eventually."

Stories Yet to Be Told

Pride & Joy: LGBTQ Artists, Icons and Everday Heroes is just the beginning of a conversation about how queer citizens of the world can live happy, successful, fulfilling lives out and proud. You, dear reader, are part of the discussion. From around the corner or around the globe, I welcome your story. Go to www.kathleenarchambeau.com and begin a dialogue with queer artists, icons, and everyday heroes from every paddock, every city street, every rural route, every suburban housing development, every apartment building, every sports field, every stage, every school, every university, every work space, every pulpit, every government body, every country, every home on the planet. Your story may inspire a queer teen to come out to their parents or a queer professional to come out at work. Your story may inspire a couple to marry or start a family. Your story may move a straight audience to see the full humanity of LGBTQ people and empathize with the real lives we live. Your story may overcome prejudice and discrimination. Your story may

change a law. Your story may
stop a hate crime. Your story may
save a life.

"Your story may
overcome prejudice and
discrimination. Your
story may change a law.
Your story may stop a
hate crime. Your story
may save a life."

Kathleen Archambeau

Nonprofit Organizations Benefiting From Sale of *Pride & Joy: LGBTQ Artists, Icons and Everyday Heroes*

Nonprofit Organizations Benefiting From Sale of
Pride & Joy: LGBTQ Artists, Icons and Everyday Heroes

A percentage of the net proceeds of sale of this book will be distributed to one or more of the following nonprofit organizations featured in this book:

- **www.freshmeatproductions.org**: Transgender and Queer Arts: Sean Dorsey

- **www.newyorklivearts.org**: Body Arts Organization, Chelsea, NYC; Bill T. Jones

- **www.ohanaarts.org**: Fostering peace through the universal language of the arts; Laurie Rubin

- **www.ballroombasix.org**: Fun, Fitness and Fancy Footwork, Harlem, NYC; Sidney Grant

- **www.nclrights.org**: Achieving LGBT Equality Through Litigation, Legislation, Policy, and Public Education; Kate Kendell

- **www.rmnetwork.org**: Reconciling Ministries; UMC Bishop Dr. Karen Oliveto

- **www.lesbianswhotech.org**: Leanne Pittsford

- **www.ccsf.edu**: Lesbian, Gay, Bisexual and Transgender Studies Department; Dr. Ardel Thomas

- **www.mwwl.org.nz**: Maori Women's Welfare League; Louisa Wall

- **www.glad.org**: Legal Advocates & Defenders for the LGBTQ Community; John "LongJones" Abdallah Wambere

- **www.nba.com/warriors/foundation**: Golden State Warriors Community Foundation; Rick Welts

Please consider donating to an organization that resonates with you.

LGBTQ Resources

www.thetrevorproject.org: Crisis Intervention and Suicide Prevention for LGBTQ Youth

https://bornthisway.foundation/: Empowering Youth, Inspiring Bravery

www.transequality.org: National Center for Transgender Equality

www.nclrights.org: National Center for Lesbian Rights

www.hrc.org: Human Rights Campaign, Strengthening the Fight for Equal Rights

www.outandequal.org: Workplace Equality

www.lesbianswhotech.org, Lesbians in Technology

www.ourfamily.org: Our Family Coalition, LGBTQ Parenting Support and Programs

www.immigrationequality.org: Protecting Families, Empowering Immigrants

www.pflag.org: Information, Support, Tools and Resources for Parents and Friends of Lesbians and Gays

www.glsen.org: Gay, Lesbian, Straight Education Network, Championing LGBTQ issues in K-12 education

www.outrightinternational.org: LGBTQ advocacy and human rights education around the world

www.spectrumuganda.net: Spectrum Uganda, gay men's health programs and initiatives

www.unfe.org: United Nations Free and Equal, Freedom and Equality Globally regardless of Sexual Orientation or Gender Identity

www.itgetsbetter.org: It Gets Better Project, communicate to LGBTQ youth around the world that It Gets Better

www.glaad.org/mediaawards: GLAAD Media Awards recognize the fair, accurate and inclusive representations of the LGBTQ Community

About the Author

Kathleen Archambeau is an award-winning writer and longtime LGBTQ activist. A native San Franciscan, she was a founding contributor to the James Hormel LGBT wing of the San Francisco Public Library. As Vice President and Co-Chair of the Fundraising Committee of the Board of Directors of Operation Concern, one of the oldest and largest mental health agencies serving the LGBT community, she was given an Outstanding Service Award. With her Kiwi wife, Kathleen Archambeau competed and won two Bronze Medals in Ballroom Dancing at the Gay Games in Cologne, Germany. Archambeau contributed a regular column profiling LGBTQ artists in one of the longest-running LGBTQ publications in the US, the *San Francisco Bay Times*. Archambeau's first book, *Climbing the Corporate Ladder in High Heels,* was featured in *Forbes* twice, endorsed by US House of Representatives Majority Leader Nancy Pelosi, and CEO and Chair of BareEscentuals, Leslie Blodgett; it has been translated into Chinese, Korean, Lithuanian, and Portuguese. Her

essay, "Seized," one of only two
lesbian creative nonfiction entries
in a collection of twenty-one
authors, including Pulitzer Prize
winner Jane Smiley, entitled,
The Other Woman, edited
by Victoria Zackheim, was
lauded by *Publishers Weekly*
for its " "top-drawer writers."
Kathleen Archambeau studied
with National Book Award
winner, poet Adrienne Rich;
American Book Award winner,
Elizabeth Woody; and Nobel
Prize for Literature winner, Derek
Walcott. She was a Department
of Education Fellow at the
University of Iowa and is a
legacy donor focused on LGBTQ
writers for the University of Iowa
Writers Workshop. She lives
with her wife and Guide Dog
Career Change Puppy in the San
Francisco Bay Area.